SMALL
BUSINESS
STREET
SMARTS

Published by

The Advertising Department Pty. Ltd.

ACN 003 519 631

FOURTH EDITION REVISED 1997
First published in 1992 © Peter Thorpe

Published by:
The Advertising Department Pty. Ltd.
A.C.N. 003 519 631
7th floor 8 Kippax Street
SURRY HILLS 2010
Australia

Tel (02) 9282 6937 Fax (02) 9211 2359

ISBN 0 646 12569 9

Printed in Australia by McPherson's Printing Group, Victoria.

Cartoons by Paul Dorin

Edited by Liz Hutley

Publishers note:
Every effort has been made to ensure that the information contained in this book is accurate and free from omissions and error. However, the publisher and author cannot be held responsible for any injury, loss or damage occasioned by any actions or lack of actions, as a result of the material contained in this book. Any advice contained within is of a general nature and should not be substituted for professional advice.

SMALL BUSINESS STREET SMARTS

by Peter Thorpe

A guide to starting and
running a successful
small business in Australia.

ABOUT THE AUTHOR...

Peter Thorpe's experience in business spans over thirty years and during that time he has held a number of top management positions including that of general manager of Sharp Corporation of Australia. For the last 20 years he has operated his own business in the fields of importing, retailing, advertising and publishing.

In 1988, he saw an opportunity to capitalise on his extensive knowledge of running a business and started his own national magazine called *Australian Small Business Review* (now called *In Business*). The publication, which was largely based on his own personal findings, was an outstanding success and he was ultimately bought out by a large publishing house.

Today, he runs his own training and consulting business called *Peter Thorpe Marketing*. He advises and consults to some of Australia's leading companies on the topics of business development, strategy planning and sales and marketing.

He is a former NSW state president of SWAP *(Salespeople With a Purpose)* and a sought after keynote speaker on the topics of business development, marketing and entrepreneurial skills.

Also by the same author...

ONE TO ONE MARKETING
Co-produced with direct marketing expert Ian Kennedy, this program consists of six audio cassette tapes and a workbook. It features ideas and information on marketing for businesses.

BE YOUR OWN BOSS - THE VIDEO
A two and a half hour workshop on video, complete with workbook. Ideal for business starters or as a valuable training resource for trainers in business management and entrepreneurial skills. *Note: This product is now available in Cantonese, Mandarin, Vietnamese and Indonesian language versions.*

For information about the above programs phone (02) 9282 6937.

WHY I WROTE THIS BOOK

With literally hundreds of books already on the market about starting and running a small business, why write another one?

Simply because most of them have been written by accountants and academics, some of whom have never actually been in business for themselves! As a result of this most of them tend to concentrate far too much on the bookkeeping and record keeping side and not enough on dealing with the every day problems encountered in running a small business.

Let me stress that I am not knocking accountants; they play a vital role in the success of any small business; and of course record keeping and bookkeeping are very important aspects and they shouldn't be overlooked. But the truth is, only a relatively small percentage of businesses fail as a direct result of poor record keeping. Furthermore, it is usually one of the easiest problems to fix; if you have a good business that is generating healthy profits, it is relatively easy and inexpensive to get outside assistance in this area.

This book is not intended to be a textbook in the classic sense of the word (although most of the main points are covered). It is aimed at combining the basic information with what I call the 'street smarts' of small business; the things that they don't always tell you about in the textbooks.

I have spent almost twenty years running various types of businesses and I have enjoyed some notable successes. However, I have also had my share of setbacks and I once owned a business that failed, resulting in my losing virtually every penny that I had in the world. It was a dreadful experience and one that I would not recommend to anybody.

Unfortunately, every year thousands of small business owners in Australia suffer a similar fate. If sharing my experiences through this book results in even one of these failures being avoided, then the time and effort put into writing it will have been well worthwhile. I trust you find it helpful and I wish you good luck with your business.

Peter Thorpe

CONTENTS

SECTION ONE: STARTING OUT

SECTION TWO: MANAGEMENT

SECTION THREE:
SALES, ADVERTISING & PROMOTION

SECTION ONE:

STARTING OUT

1. WHY DO SO MANY SMALL BUSINESSES FAIL?

"No one ever achieved worthwhile success who did not, at one time or another, find himself with at least one foot hanging well over the brink of failure."
Napoleon Hill

Firstly, let me start out by saying this is not a book about failure, this is a book about success - *your success!* It is a book about how to make *your* small business not only survive but thrive and grow. For this reason I was very reluctant to start out on a negative note; however, the alarmingly high rate of small business failure in Australia is well documented and it would be foolish for me or you to ignore it. Starting and running a successful small business is no easy task and it is going to require a lot of hard work and dedication on your part. Anybody who is planning to start their own business thinking they are in for an easy ride, would be wise to think again.

Having said that, here is the good news: there is nothing more exhilarating and rewarding than running your own successful business. The sense of achievement combined with the feeling of self-satisfaction that comes from being in charge of your own destiny, are well and truly worth the effort. So, let's deal with the negative factors first and get them out of the way so that we can concentrate on the positive aspects of making your business a success.

What makes a business successful?
In order to find out what makes a business successful, we must first take a look at what causes them to fail. Through this process we can learn what the most common mistakes are and how to avoid them.

Surprisingly little research has been conducted into small business failure and, more importantly, the reasons they fail. The most commonly quoted figures on small business failure are those from a study undertaken by Professor Alan Williams of the Newcastle University. His research indicated that about 32 per cent of new business startups fail within the first year and around 75 per cent fail within five years. A new research program is currently underway to update these figures but no matter what the findings are, suffice to say that the number of small businesses that fail in Australia is frightfully high and anyone considering going into business for themselves would be well advised to think long and hard before taking the plunge.

The main causes of small business failure

While the precise causes are often difficult to define, by far the largest number of small business failures are directly attributable to poor management and lack of expertise. A relatively small percentage of businesses actually fail due to outside factors, such as union problems or government policies, etc. While these issues can certainly be a factor, it could also be argued that good management would have taken these outside factors into consideration and had a contingency plan.

In any analysis of small business failure, there are a number of common mistakes that appear time and again. Here are some of the more common ones:

Failure to plan

Thorough planning and adequate research into the potential of the business venture are absolutely essential. Many people start out in business on little more than a whim and and a prayer, thinking they can learn 'on-the-job' as they go along. The classic 'She'll be right, mate' approach.

Well, unfortunately, she definitely won't be right! It's a hard, cruel world out there and there are very few second chances, especially in a tough business climate. When we have a booming economy and rapid growth it is much easier to start a successful business. In tough times there is a lot less margin for error and it is even more important that you get it right the first time.

14

Lack of capital

Often people underestimate the total cost of setting up a business and don't take into account the massive expense involved in just getting to the stage where they can open the doors for trading. Some consider only the setting up costs and don't allow a sufficient period of time to start generating an income. While there will always be some unforeseen expenses, this problem can usually be avoided by having a thorough business plan which includes a projected cash flow analysis *(see chapters on Business Planning)*.

Partnership problems

Making a partnership work effectively is a very difficult task. Potential partners need to be selected with extreme care. There is an old adage that says "you don't really know someone until you live with them." This could be adapted in the business world to: "you don't really know somebody until you go into partnership with them!" *(See chapter on Partnerships.)*

Wrong pricing structure

Another common mistake is failure to price the product or service correctly. Many small business operators go broke simply because they underprice themselves. Overpricing can be a problem too but from my experience, underpricing is by far the most common mistake. *(See chapter on Pricing for Profit).*

Failure to seek and/or take advice

Many small business starters see legal and accounting advice and training in managerial skills as too expensive and not totally necessary. While capital is precious when you start up, a few dollars spent at the outset can save you thousands later on. A wise man once said, "If you think the price of knowledge is expensive, you should try the price of ignorance!"

Credit problems and bad debts

A sale is not a sale until you have been paid! Too many small business operators fail to take sufficient steps to make sure they get paid. The business graveyard is full of firms that went broke because they extended credit to other companies and didn't get paid themselves!

Neglect

Many a small business goes to the wall simply because the owners don't spend enough time in the business. Don't even think about going into business for yourself unless you are prepared to work hard and for long hours, particularly in the formative years. Your business is your baby and you must keep a careful eye on it at all times. You wouldn't leave your baby in the care of total strangers, would you? Take the same care with your business.

Marketing problems

Another common reason a lot of small businesses fail is simply because they don't make sufficient sales. Not enough emphasis is placed on the importance of marketing. Knowing your market and what it requires is vital to your survival. Unfortunately, many of the books written about starting and running a small business concentrate far too much on the record keeping and accountancy side and not enough on the marketing aspects. While the former is very important, marketing is often the make or break of a business venture. After all, if you don't make enough sales you won't need to keep records - *you will go broke!* It's as simple as that.

Failure to remain 'hands on'

As a business grows and develops, it is not uncommon to see the person or persons who created the business become involved in activities that are either totally foreign to the business or relatively unimportant to it. Don't be afraid to delegate tasks that can be performed by somebody else, freeing you up to do what you do best, but make sure that you don't lose touch with your business.

Most small business failure could be avoided

The saddest thing about small business failure is the fact that most of them could be avoided if the persons going into the business simply took the time and effort to prepare themselves for the task ahead. Far too many people plunge straight into the deep end, with little or no training. Many have had no previous experience in the industry they are entering. In spite of this, they often risk everything they own on their ability to scrape through. This inevitably involves more than just monetary risks. It can also mean ruining your health, the break-

16

down of a marriage, the loss of friends and personal self-esteem.

Careful planning and training can dramatically reduce your chances of failure. Running your own successful business can be a most rewarding and satisfying experience. It can also offer a lot more long-term security than working for someone else, because you are in charge of your own destiny. Most successful small business operators would never go back to working for a boss. So do your homework thoroughly and make sure you don't become one of the failure statistics. *So remember, don't fail to plan - plan to succeed!*

2. ARE YOU SUITED TO GOING INTO BUSINESS FOR YOURSELF?

"The two most important ingredients for success in business are: common sense and a sense of humour."
Mark McCormack, author of the book, *Things They Don't Teach You at Harvard Business School.*

There are really no hard and fast rules for the right type of personality for self-employment. After all, there are so many different businesses you can choose from and the personality traits required vary greatly from industry to industry. I have seen people whom I thought would surely fail, go on to achieve great success and people whom I thought would be outstandingly successful fail dismally. However, I must say that these cases are more the exception than the rule.

While it is difficult to predict with any accuracy an individual's chances of success or failure based purely on attitudinal or personality traits, there are some common attributes that can be associated with successful business operators. Below, I have assigned ratings points to what I feel are the eight most important ingredients for success in running your own business, for you to rate yourself against. They are based mainly on my personal observations of what makes a successful small business person. They are not a test and there is no pass or failure mark. It is included in the book to simply make you aware of any areas that may need improvement.

How it works
Each of the eight attributes listed is represented by a spoke in a wheel (see figure 1 page 21). Rate your score on a scale of none to ten and make a mark on each spoke of the wheel where you think you rate. The smallest wheel represents nil and the largest (outer) wheel represents ten. Finally, join up the marks to form a continuous line. This then becomes your personal wheel of business success.

The larger your wheel, the better it runs. If your wheel has large bumps or dips in it *(see figure 2 page 22)* try to improve these areas to smooth out your wheel and get it running better.

Attributes and scoring method:

Spoke A. Health
What state of health do you normally enjoy?

excellent	8 - 10
pretty good	5 - 7
average to poor	2 - 4
not too good	0 - 1

Spoke B. Family support
Do you have the support of your family?

behind me 100%	8 - 10
most of them behind me	5 - 7
not very supportive	2 - 4
totally against it	0 - 1

Spoke C. Self esteem
How do you rate your chances of success in business, based on your knowledge of your own ability?

extremely confident	8 - 10
reasonably confident	5 - 7
not sure	2 - 4
very unsure	0 - 1

Spoke D. Industry experience
What is your experience in the industry chosen?

Extensive experience	8 - 10
some experience	5 - 7
very little experience	2 - 4
no experience at all	0 - 1

Spoke E. Management experience
What previous management experience have you had?

extensive experience at high level	8 - 10
some management experience	5 - 7
very little management experience	2 - 4
no previous management experience	0 - 1

Spoke F. Capacity for hard work
How hard are you prepared to work in your own business?

as hard as it requires to succeed	8 - 10
harder than I work now	5 - 7
hoping to do less than present job	2 - 4
looking for an easier life	0 -1

Spoke G. Enthusiasm
How enthusiastic are you about starting out in business?

extremely enthusiastic	8 - 10
very enthusiastic	5 - 7
mildly enthusiastic	2 - 4
not looking forward to it	0 - 1

Spoke H. Preparation
*How would you describe your preparedness for the task ahead?
Have you really done your homework and prepared a thorough
business plan?*

extremely well prepared	8 - 10
quite well prepared	5 - 7
not very well prepared	2 - 4
no preparation at all	0 - 1

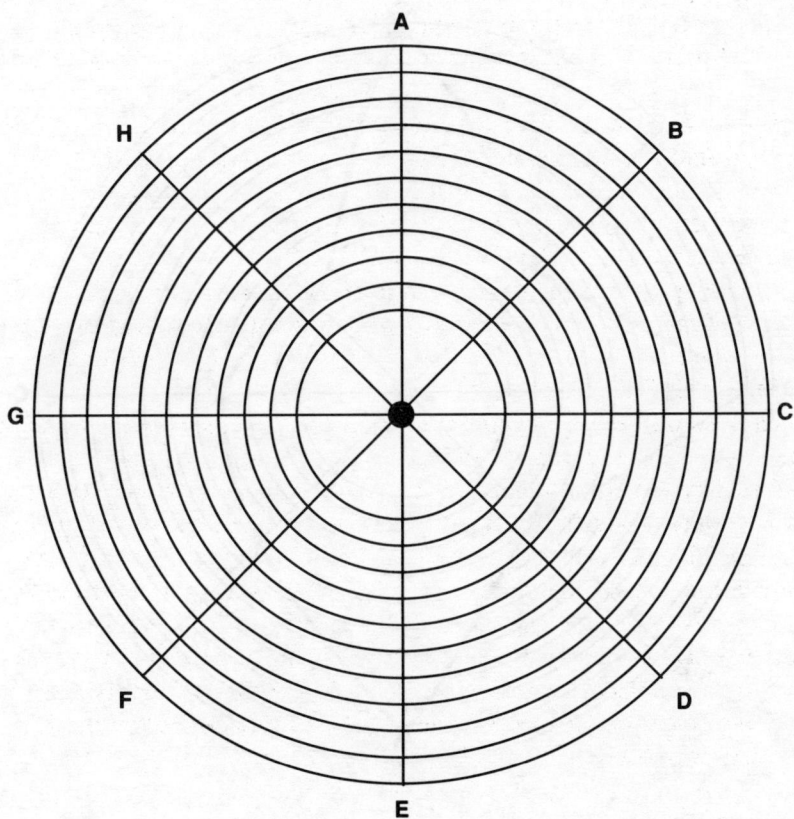

Figure 1.

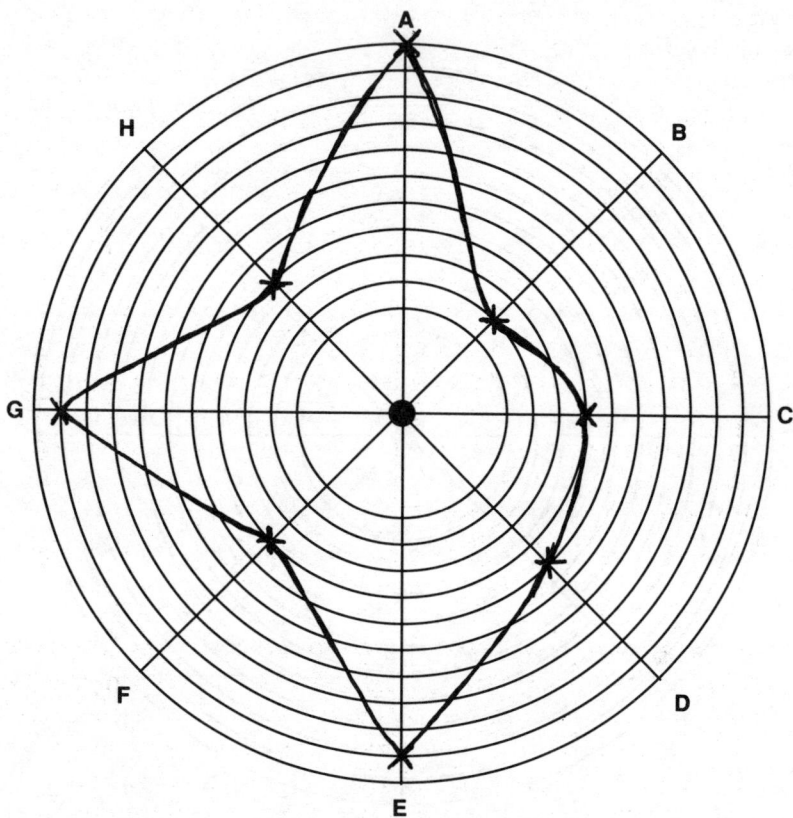

Figure 2. If your wheel looks like this, it won't run very well at all. Work on improving your areas of weakness.

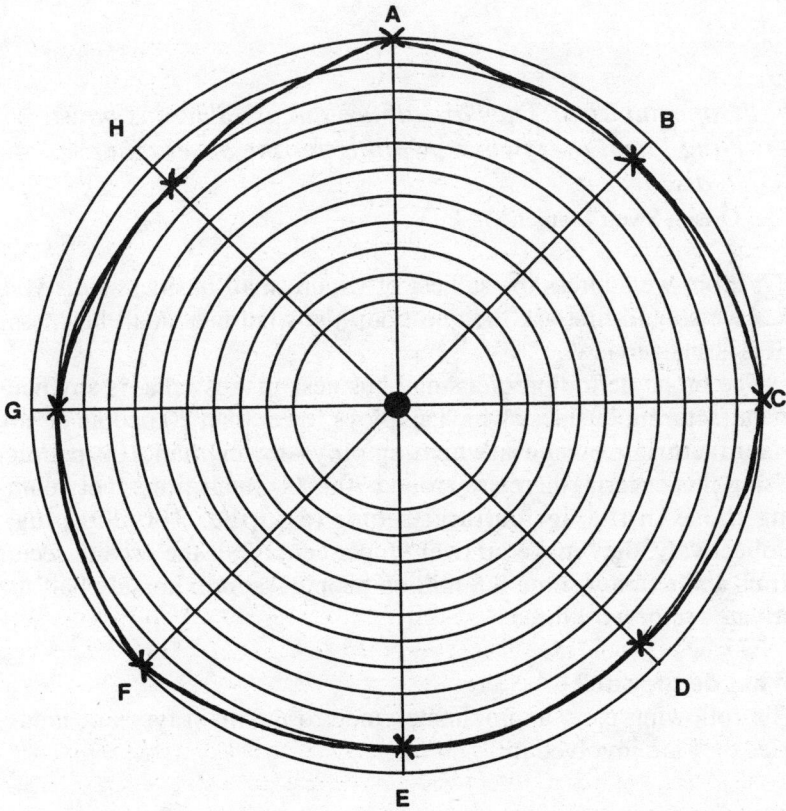

Figure 3. If your wheel has the odd bump or lump in it, it will still run okay but you may be in for a bumpy ride! Work on improving your weak spots.

3. WHICH BUSINESS IS FOR YOU?

"Opportunities? They are all around us...There is power lying latent everywhere, waiting for the observant eye to discover it."
Orison Swett Marden

Before we address the subject of which small business suits you, we should first ask the question: just what is a small business? Here is an overview:

The broad definition of a small business in Australia, is any non-manufacturing business which employs fewer than 20 people or any manufacturing business which employs fewer than 100 people. Using this criteria, there are around 700,000 small firms, not counting those in the agricultural sector (a further 100,000 plus). Collectively, they make up over 96 per cent of all the private sector firms and employ some 2.5 million people - approximately half the private sector workforce.

What do they do?
The following is an approximate guide to the main types of industries they are involved in:

manufacturing	9
construction	20
wholesale trade	7
retail trade	21
transport and storage	7
finance, property and business services	16
community service	9
recreational, personal and other services	11
	=====
total	100%

Women in business

Despite women's liberation and the fact that women are taking over more of the so called *'traditional men's roles'* in society, it appears that to date, women entrepreneurs in Australia are still fairly thin on the ground.

It is often quoted that approximately one third of all the small businesses in Australia are controlled by women however, this is simply not true. Relatively few women play the *leading* role in managing a small business, despite the fact that they are involved in 56 per cent of all small businesses.

According to the Yellow Pages Small Business Index™ *(1996)* women play the leading role in only around 13 per cent of all the businesses in Australia and share the leading role in a further 19 per cent. The balance of 68 per cent per cent of all businesses are controlled solely by men.

So, why are there so few women who are prepared to take up the challenge? *It just doesn't make sense.* Women who work in big companies today, still complain about the *'glass ceiling syndrome'*. This is the invisible barrier that many women claim stops them rising to the top in a corporate world which is still largely dominated by men. The fact remains, most women will have to work for themselves, if they want to realise their full potential.

Perhaps the lack of women entrepreneurs can be attributed to the fact that there still seems to be a fair degree of prejudice against women business owners. And, financiers have tended to place restrictions on would-be women entrepreneurs when it comes to lending for business. Hopefully, this is changing.

After all, there is no reason why women can't run businesses just as well (or even better in some cases) than men. Women have all the right attributes to be successful.

So, come on girls, what are you waiting for?

Why go into business?

Let's get back to the subject (regardless of your sex) of trying to determine which type of business is best for you. The first question you should ask yourself is:

"Why do I want to go into my own business in the first place?"

Most people usually want to start their own business for three major reasons:

- *To make more money than they can make working for somebody else.*
- *To be independent and in control of their own destiny.*
- *For security of long-term employment.*

Many people start their own business for all the *wrong* reasons. Here is a short list of some of the *don'ts*.

Don't start your own business because:

- *You think you are going to have an easy life with someone else doing all the work.*
- *You have a hobby or interest and you think it would be a fun way to earn a living.*
- *You just feel you need a change in your employment.*
- *You are unemployed and feel you have to buy yourself a job.*
- *Somebody else said you would be good at it.*

All of the above may seem like good enough reasons to start your own business but none of them on their own are sufficient to guarantee your success. Do consider starting out in business for yourself if you have any or all of the following attributes:

- *You are a high achiever and feel you could do better for yourself.*
- *You are a hard worker and are prepared to work long and hard to make it succeed.*
- *You are a positive, entrepreneurial type, with lots of energy and bright ideas and feel you are being stifled by your present employer.*
- *You have a strong desire to build a better future for yourself and your family.*

Which business is for you?

You should put a great deal of thought into this question because you are probably going to spend a lot of time doing whatever it is you finally decide to do. Take into account the following points before making your final decision:

What is your level of experience in the industry chosen?
Do you have sufficient knowledge, experience and industry contacts to be successful?

Do you have sufficient capital?
Not only to buy or set up the business but also to carry you through until you start to generate an income?

Do you have the right temperament for the business?
For instance, if you are going to be dealing with the general public all day in a retail situation, do you genuinely enjoy meeting people? Do you usually get along well with strangers?

Is it something you will enjoy doing?
You will have a far greater chance of being successful if you choose something you like doing.

Are the hours of operating the business suitable to your lifestyle?
For instance, if it requires a lot of weekend work, are you prepared to sacrifice your leisure time?

> *Note: No matter what business you go into, you will probably be working a great deal more than the 'normal' 38-hour working week. If you are not prepared to do this, you should question your suitability to go into business for yourself. Maybe you would be better off working for somebody else?*

Do you have the support of your family?
Are your family behind you all the way or are they very reluctant? *A word of warning:* Don't confuse this reluctance with healthy scepticism or caution. It is natural for a spouse or relative to worry about

27

the security aspects and the possibility of losing everything you own. If you are married, it is important that your spouse sees your business venture as a calculated risk and that they believe in what you are trying to achieve. If the going gets tough (and there is a good chance that it will, particularly in the early stages) the last thing you will need is the additional pressure of your spouse saying: *"I told you so!"*

If your spouse is totally against the idea and you can't get him or her to share your enthusiasm for the project, it would probably be better for all concerned if you reconsidered. Perhaps they have an insight into weaknesses in you or your plan that you may not have considered. Try to enlist the advice of an outsider, preferably someone whom you both know and respect, to review the plans with you together. While it is still possible to succeed without the support of your spouse or family, it will certainly make life a lot easier if you have their blessings.

Summary
Before making a commitment, talk to as many people as you can, especially other people in their own business. Ask them to tell you about their findings and experiences, both good and bad. Most people are only too willing to share them with you.

Think long and hard before choosing which business you are going to enter. It will probably be one of the most important decisions you make in your life, so don't rush it.

4. BUYING AN ESTABLISHED BUSINESS

"Business is a game, the greatest game in the world if you know how to play it."

Thomas J. Watson

Once you have made the decision to go into business, your next question is likely to be: *"should I buy an existing business or should I start from scratch?"*

There are a number of advantages in buying a business that has been in operation for some time. A customer or client base already exists, therefore you should be able to assess future turnover and profit, and (very important) you have access to an immediate cash flow and income.

Of course, you will be expected to pay for this privilege. This usually takes the form of a payment for the business itself (plant, equipment and stock) plus a payment for what is called *goodwill*. Just how to assess the worth of this goodwill can be a complex issue. More on that later but first, let's quickly have a look at some of the pros and cons of buying an established business.

The major benefits can be summed up as follows:

- *proven track record increasing the likelihood of success*
- *immediate cash flow and income generated from existing established customer base*
- *easier to arrange finance on a proven concept (however, the amount required is likely to be a good deal more than the cost of a new startup, so you may require more capital)*
- *sometimes experienced staff are happy to stay on with the new owner*

- *the purchaser may be able to arrange for the vendor to stay on for a while to train them in the operation of the business*
- *the problem of selecting the wrong location is minimised*
- *lines of credit with suppliers are already established*
- *choice of stock items is already determined*
- *plant and equipment may be available at a greatly written down cost*
- *the suitability and capability of equipment is already known.*

When buying an established business you should ask the following questions:

- *are you buying at a fair price or are you paying too much for the goodwill?*
- *are the figures presented a genuine picture of the business and can this be expected to continue into the long-term future?*
- *can you be assured that the business will continue to perform as promised under the new ownership?*
- *is the plant and equipment offered on the way out and in need of replacement at a high cost?*
- *are there any unknown factors that will adversely affect the business in the future, such as a major competitor about to open nearby or the closure of a main roadway?*
- *are there any government regulations or laws about to change that will affect the business?*
- *is the business based on a passing trend or fad that is about to change for the worse?*

These are just a few of the problems and questions facing the intending purchaser. The Small Business Development Corporation in your state puts out a checklist of over 40 points to look out for when buying an established business. Get a copy of this and seek advice from an expert.

Goodwill

If you are going to buy an established business, you will generally be asked to make a payment for the goodwill. So, just what is goodwill and how much should you expect to pay for it?

Generally speaking, goodwill is an intangible thing. It is not something you can hold in your hand. It may be the methodology of a manufacturing process or it could be the rights to some sort of exclusive location or territory. Usually it involves the right to take over an existing client base and continue the business, enjoying at least the same level of sales and profits as the previous owner. Of course, this is always subject to question.

The seller of a business often perceives the worth of the goodwill to be much higher than it really is and the buyer sees it as being less than it is. The reality usually lies somewhere in the middle. Banks and other financial institutions are reluctant to lend money on goodwill because of the difficulty in assessing its true worth and the possible inability of the new owner to be able to realise this *'asset'* especially in a forced sale.

Problems could also arise if the business has been built through some special expertise which can't or won't be easily passed on. In the case of a restaurant for example, the personality of the previous owner or their extraordinary cooking ability may have attracted a large following. Perhaps the new owners will not be able to duplicate this. Maybe when the old owner leaves the customers will follow, perhaps to his or her new business. This can be overcome to some extent with non-compete clauses in the contract of sale but be warned: *these are becoming harder and harder to enforce.* Courts are reluctant to deny people the right to earn a living.

Calculation of goodwill

There are numerous different methods of calculating goodwill and some are more suited to certain types of businesses than others. How you measure the goodwill of a hotel for instance, would be totally different to the method used to measure the goodwill of a lawn mowing run.

Many different factors need to be taken into account. In the first instance, you should calculate what would be a fair return on the capital that will be tied up in the business, plus a fair wage for you. *Note:* Return on capital would need to be substantially higher than what you could expect to get if you simply invested the money in a bank or bonds, etc. Because of the high degree of risk, you should expect to get a return that is substantially higher than the current

31

rate on a reasonably safe investment. You should then calculate what would be a fair wage for running the business. For instance, how much would you have to pay a manager to run the business for you or how much would you expect to be paid if you were running the business for wages?

Once these factors have been accounted for, any net profits above these amounts are what is called *super profits*. These are generally used as the benchmark to calculate the worth of the goodwill of the business.

Here is an example:

A. amount of capital invested in the business	100,000
B. expected return on capital invested (at say 10%)	10,000
C. fair wage for you for running the business, say	40,000
D. anticipated fair return on capital invested plus a fair wage (B + C)	50,000
E. anticipated net operating profit (after running expenses but before tax)	100,000
less fair return (D) (minus)	- 50,000
	========
anticipated super profit	50,000

In the above scenario your super profit would be $50,000. This figure then becomes the yardstick for calculating the worth of the goodwill of the business.

There is no hard and fast rule for calculating the multiplying factor for goodwill, and it is affected by many things. For instance, how long has the business been established and can it be reasonably expected that the profits will continue at the present rate? What is the degree of exclusivity and how long can that be expected to continue? If you can't forecast these with any certainty for more than one year, then the goodwill may not be worth much at all. If, on the other hand you can expect them to continue long term, goodwill may be worth three or four times the super profit amount or even more in some circumstances. In business however, predicting the future with any great degree of certainty is a precarious occupation. From my own experience, very few businesses have a goodwill value of more than one year's super profit and I would adopt this as your yardstick. And remember, any calculation of goodwill should always err on the conservative side.

WARNING: Be extremely careful when assessing the value of goodwill.

It is wise to seek the advice of both an accountant and solicitor, both with extensive experience in the chosen industry. A good friend of mine, Max Hitchins, a well-known hotel broker, told me recently of a case where an accountant advised a purchaser that the returns on a particular hotel looked quite good. Max claims that by industry standards, they were in fact quite poor and well below what would be accepted by that industry as *'normal'*. The accountant had had no previous experience in the hotel business. Consequently, the purchaser paid far more for the business than it was worth.

One final word of caution on evaluating goodwill. Be very careful of people who quote figures in so called *'black money'* or *'under the counter'* money. It is quite common for people selling businesses (particularly cash businesses) to talk about the hidden amount of money that doesn't go through the books, thereby avoiding the scrutiny of the taxman. And of course, because there is no record kept of this imaginary money, you usually have no way of checking whether it really exists.

Recent changes to the law now oblige accountants and business brokers to make the Taxation Department aware of such practices and there are very hefty fines and possible imprisonment for offenders, consequently the practice is much less common these days however, I have no doubt that it still goes on. My advice to an intending purchaser would be to leave this type of thing out of your calculations altogether. Unless you can see it in the books in black and white, chances are it's not there anyway. Work on the principle: *If in doubt - leave it out!*

Summary

In the final analysis, the amount you pay for goodwill should be weighed against starting up an identical business from scratch.

There are some clear advantages to starting out from scratch, such as being able to select the location and introduce your own personal touch to the business however, you will find raising finance a much bigger problem and the high cost of trial and error may be greater than paying the price for an existing business with an established clientelle and cash flow. With a new start up, you may also have to face the problem of a long period of time with little or no income.

Either way, it is a very difficult decision and one you should give a great deal of thought to. Seek the advice of your *'three wise men' (or women)* - your accountant, your bank manager and your solicitor. If it is at all possible, find somebody with experience in the business you have chosen to enter, who is prepared to give you an unbiased assessment. *Ask them - would they buy the business themselves?*

5. WHICH BUSINESS STRUCTURE SHOULD YOU USE?

"Many a man has taken the first step. With every additional step you enhance immensely the value of your first."

Ralph Waldo Emerson

Whether you are setting up a new business or taking over an existing one, you must first decide which type of structure you are going to operate the business under. There are a number of options, the most common ones being:

- *sole trader*
- *company*
- *partnership*
- *trust*

The decision as to which one you use should not be entered into lightly, as it may have far reaching implications later on and could affect such things as capital gains considerations, should you decide to sell the business or take in a partner. It can also have a dramatic effect on how much tax you are liable for.

The type of structure you use will depend on your individual situation and it is advisable to talk to your solicitor and accountant about the options available to you before you start. However, as with most legal matters, it is prudent to have a reasonable working knowledge of the types of structures available and how they operate before seeking advice. This will save you *time* and *money*.

What follows is a general look at the various structures and their advantages and disadvantages. There are a number of aspects that need to be considered. These include:

- *taxation (how to minimise the amount you pay)*
- *capital gains tax considerations and income splitting opportunities*
- *the cost vs benefits of running the structure (Note: it is important to consider ongoing costs as well as setting up costs)*
- *aspects of the limited liability of the individuals involved*
- *any legislation which might limit your choice of structure*
- *any adverse effects on the prospects of raising finance for the venture*
- *the implications of having to pay provisional tax.*

On the next page you will find an overview of the most common structures. It must be stressed that the laws involved (both state and federal) change from time to time and this information should be used as a guide only.

TYPES OF STRUCTURES*

	ADVANTAGES	DISADVANTAGES
SOLE TRADER	low cost of entry	*personal liabilty*
	easy to set up	*for all debts*
	no big legal costs	
		need to pay
		provisional tax
	no separate tax	
	return required	
		when you die, it dies
	no registration required	
	(if using your own name)	
PARTNERSHIP	partnership itself	*personal liability*
	does not pay tax	*for all debts*
		liability for other
	relatively inexpensive	*partners' debts & actions*
	to set up and run although	
	agreement needed	*relationship problems*
COMPANY	limited liability	*expensive to set up and run*
	(now greatly reduced)	
		separate tax and company
	income splitting opportunities	*returns required*
		knowledge of director's
		responsibilities needed
TRUSTS	income sharing with family	*expensive to set up and run*
	(now somewhat limited)	
		complicated to administer
		disgruntled relatives
		may sue later

* The above information is intended as a guide only and should not be a substitute for legal advice.

Here is a brief overview of each of the structures:

Sole trader

There are a number of advantages with being a sole trader and these days, with the reduction of limited liability for company directors plus the mounting costs and complexity of compliance for companies, it is well worth considering this alternative. If you do decide to trade under your own name there is no need to even register your business name, i.e. if your name is John Smith and you decide to use that as your trading name, there is no legal requirement to register that name. If, however, you decide to use the name *John Smith Television Repairs* or *John Smith's Record Bar* you will need to register your name with the Corporate Affairs office in your state. A small fee is payable initially, followed by a periodical renewal fee.

> *Note: A registered business name is not a company, it is simply the registration of your chosen trading name which prevents anyone else from using the same name.*

If you do decide to form a company you will be required to use the words Pty. Ltd. after your business name, e.g. *John Smith's Record Bar Pty. Ltd.* or *Pty. Limited.* You can register a business name in the name of a company and then trade under that business name. e.g. *XYZ & Co. Pty. Ltd., trading as John Smith's Record Bar* but you are required to spell out your full trading name as well as your company name and number on all documentation and as you can see, it becomes quite long winded and is therefore not recommended.

The major disadvantage of being a sole trader is, you are personally liable for all debts incurred in the business name, just as if you had incurred them in your own name. In the event of the business failing, your creditors have full rights to claim against your assets, such as your home, your car, virtually anything you own of value.

While this may sound pretty drastic, it is worth bearing in mind that even if you have a company structure you may still find yourself signing personal guarantees for loans and goods and services extended to you on credit. In the final analysis, this may well have the same effect as being a sole trader (so far as personal liability is concerned). You should discuss the benefits both ways with your solicitor and accountant and based on their advice, make a valued judgment as to whether the expense of forming and running a company is warranted. If you are not going to incur large trade debtors it may well be easier and cheaper to trade as a sole trader or partnership.

Company structure

The most popular way of starting up a company is to buy what is known as a *shelf company* and then change its name. Shelf companies are companies that have been formed, usually by solicitors and then literally *'put on a shelf'* waiting for somebody to come along and buy them.

The advantage of this system is, it is usually quicker than forming a company from scratch and because the solicitors involved virtually package these company structures in bulk, it generally works out cheaper. Note: In their efforts to come up with names that are not already registered, shelf company names are usually made up of people's initials or some other obscure method of random selection and therefore they often sound a bit strange.

If your company is not going to have a public image you may even decide not to change the name to save costs but if you are going to be trading with the name and dealing with other people or businesses using that name, it is advisable to change the name straight away. This will avoid the confusion of changing it later on and it will also save you a considerable amount of money on items such as stationery and printed matter. Also, bear in mind it can take up to one year just to get your name listed in the telephone directories!

Note: Companies are becoming more and more expensive to run, as the various government bodies require an ever increasing amount of information and documentation. As a company, you will be required to file a separate company return with the Australian Securities Commission each year and a separate taxation return for the company, as well as your own personal income tax returns.

In theory, your liability in a company is limited to the amount outstanding on shares plus any director's or personal guarantees you have signed. Be warned however, these days more and more creditors are suing the directors of failed companies. For instance, if your company becomes insolvent (unable to meet its debts, as and when they fall due) and you as a director knowingly continue to trade, you could be held personally responsible for any debts incurred. You should also be aware that your responsibilities as a company director are quite onerous and care should be taken to exercise those responsibilities at all times.

There are a number of traps for young players with running a company and ignorance of company law is little or no defence for directors found guilty of breaching the Companies Act. Penalties are quite severe and include jail sentences as well as huge fines for breaches. Ask your solicitor and/or accountant to advise you of your responsibilities under the Act and study up on the appropriate literature.

The Australian Institute of Company Directors (a non-profit organisation) offers a range of services to members and non-members. This includes a series of courses and publications suitable for small business operators. Call the office nearest to you in your state or territory capital for further information. You'll find them listed under 'A' in your local telephone book.

Company numbers
When you form a company you are now issued with what is known as an Australian Company Number (ACN). From 1 January 1992, this number has had to appear on virtually all your paperwork. This includes your letterhead, invoices, receipts, purchase order forms, cheques, circulars, price lists and any form of legal document and the company's common seal. It must be in a legible type, no smaller than 8 point (that's this big). Make sure you include it on all the necessary documentation to avoid a fine and expensive overprinting. At time of writing the ACN is not required on business cards, with compliments slips and packaging materials.

Trusts
The main advantage of operating your business through a trust is the ability to distribute your income throughout various members of your family. Be warned however, this may have far reaching ramifications in the future. A typical example would be a situation where a family member is paid an income out of a family trust from a very

early age (possibly even birth). Later, this person becomes involved in a bitter family dispute and decides to sue the trust for his or her rightful share of the business profits over the entire life of the business. This type of incident is not uncommon and careful consideration should be given before entering into any such arrangement.

Discuss your individual situation with your solicitor and bear in mind, the solicitor could stand to gain quite a bit of money from setting up a trust. While I'm not suggesting that most solicitors will give you anything but the best advice, it can be a little bit like asking your barber if you need a haircut! Make sure you understand the full ramifications of what you are getting yourself into.

6. PARTNERSHIPS

*"When two people in business always agree,
one of them is unnecessary."*
Anon.

Of all the business structures, without doubt the most difficult to operate successfully is a partnership - be it between two people or ten people. The more people involved, the more differing opinions you will have and the more difficult they will be to resolve.

Over the years I have known a great many people involved in partnerships and I have seen very few that I could say have worked out, at least to the satisfaction of all the partners concerned. Often the partners start out as good friends and end up in bitter disputes, in some cases leading not only to the loss of the friendship, but also to the parties involved becoming mortal enemies. My advice to people considering going into a partnership in business is simple:

Don't do it if you can possibly avoid it!

Of course there are exceptions to every rule; however, if it is at all possible for you to set up the business on your own then my advice would be to do so.

The one exception to this rule is a partnership with your spouse. Having your spouse involved in your business can have distinct advantages. For starters, he or she will be more committed to the success of the venture and more likely to work for lower wages (with the expectation of better things to come). Naturally, there can still be problems and in the event of a marriage breakdown, things can become pretty messy; however the advantages will probably outweigh the disadvantages most of the time.

The main problems with partnerships usually arise out of disputes over one or more of the following:

- *who does the greatest amount of work and whether the other party is pulling their weight*
- *money problems, particularly where one partner has put in more than another*
- *spouse problems, especially where one or more of the spouses involved is working in the business*
- *management decisions, where each partner has a different idea of what needs to be done.*

The main reason people go into partnerships is to:

- *introduce more capital*
- *gain added expertise*
- *share the risks*
- *share (and thereby minimise) expenses*
- *have someone to talk to and share the problems with.*

Now, let's examine each of the above reasons and look at some of the possible alternatives:

1. To introduce more capital

I have seen people take a partner into their business for what later turns out to be a relatively insignificant amount of money. It should be remembered that the person putting in the capital could be entitled to half of the profits for the rest of the business's life! It can prove to be a very costly exercise to have to buy this person out at a later date, if things don't work out.

Alternative:
Unless the amount of capital is extensive and you really can't extend your resources any further, you may be a lot better off borrowing just a little bit more and going it alone.

2. To gain added expertise

This sounds like a good idea, especially if the person setting up the business is lacking in expertise in a particular area. However, I would question the wisdom of entering into a business partnership if you are totally dependent on the other partner for their expertise. In such an arrangement the partner with all the expertise would have an enormous advantage over the other party. Also, what if something happens to that partner? What if they become ill or get run over by a bus? *(Not a nice thought but these things do happen!)* Or in the event of a dispute or a falling out, the other partner could walk out taking all the customers and the expertise with them!

Alternative:
Consider what steps you would need to take to acquire the expertise yourself. Another alternative could be to simply employ somebody who has the expertise and at least that way, you still maintain control. If an employee proves to be unsatisfactory, you can always replace them. Note: while this latter suggestion is a better alternative, I would still question the sense in entering a business in the first place if you don't possess enough expertise to at least run the business yourself in an emergency. This is not a hard and fast rule but one well worth thinking about.

3. To share the risks

There are obvious benefits in this, however there can be just as many negatives. When you take in a partner you are also taking on responsibility for their commitments and any bad decisions they might make. You will also have another mouth to feed and you will have to share the profits with them.

Alternative:
Why not look at starting on a smaller scale and building up as you go along? Perhaps you could find somebody who is prepared to lend you the money on the promise of a high return if the venture succeeds (preferably with no recourse if the business fails). Finding such a person will depend on how attractive your business proposition is and how good a salesperson you are!

4. To share and minimise expenses
Remember, when you take other people into your business, you are also adding to your expenses. This is especially true if that extra person is going to be drawing a wage every week. It is far easier to find one wage out of a business than two.

Alternative:
If it is office or factory space you need, consider renting a serviced office or sharing premises with another business. Many businesses have more space than they need and would be happy to sublet part of their space and share expenses. If you decide on the latter, make sure they have permission to sublet from their landlord and get your solicitor to draw up an agreement to protect you from being suddenly thrown out on to the street.

5. Having someone to talk to and share the problems with
Once again, a valid reason for wanting to take in a partner but not a very sound one when you fully consider it.

Alternative:
While it is nice to have a shoulder to cry on occasionally, there are a number of options which I feel are more sensible. For starters, if you are just looking for someone to bounce ideas off, I would suggest you find a mentor. Someone who is well versed in your industry who wouldn't mind giving you advice when you need it. You may be pleasantly surprised at how many people there are like this around and the cost might be simply the odd lunch or cup of coffee or perhaps there is something you can do for them in return.

The good thing about a mentor is, you don't have to give them half of your profits and you don't have to take the advice if you don't agree with it! It is also likely that they can offer better advice because they are removed from the day-to-day running of the business and therefore are more inclined to look at the forest instead of the trees. Also they are impartial and not simply protecting their own vested interests!

Another alternative to the above is to join industry groups or your local chamber of commerce or you could even consider paying someone to give you professional advice. It could be far cheaper to pay an industry consultant for advice as needed, rather than give someone else a major share in your business.

Partnership agreements

My advice would be to study all of the above and consider the alternatives before entering into a partnership of any kind.

And if you are still determined to proceed with a partnership after all that, then at least make sure you draw up a formal partnership agreement.

This should take into account the rights and duties of all the partners involved. It should also spell out the term of the partnership, the commencement date and should include some sort of agreed method for resolving disputes. For instance, it may say that in cases where a dispute cannot be resolved by the partners, then such a dispute will be resolved by an independent arbitrator appointed by an agreed selection method (preferably by a third party). It should also make clear the liabilities of each partner and their entitlement to and share of the profits of the business. Your solicitor will be able to advise you with the wording and the main points to cover. Once again, to save time and money, have some sort of agreement between the parties drafted up before you go to visit the solicitor.

Verbal agreements

Sam Goldwyn, the Hollywood movie producer was once quoted as saying, *"Verbal contracts aren't worth the paper they're written on!"* How true!

It is quite legal to trade as a partnership without a written partnership agreement and this is quite common, especially in the case of husband and wife or other family owned businesses. However, even in a family business, it is wise to have something in writing *(perhaps even more so)* because of the possibility of a family dispute which may affect the relationship and ultimately the business. If you don't have an agreement in writing before you start, chances are you will live to regret it. I have heard many people after the event saying things like, "I just thought it was understood that he would do this or she would do that".

Remember, the best time to sort out what is expected of each partner, is before the business even starts.

47

Even if you don't need to use it for legal purposes, a partnership agreement is a good way of spelling out each partner's duties. If you don't have a written agreement in place, in the event of a dispute, you will be subject to the Partnership Act and will be forced to accept the rulings of that law.

Be warned: this Act recognises that all partners in a partnership are equal, in the absence of a written agreement to the contrary.

For taxation purposes, the partnership must file a return of income and the partners must file personal income tax returns but the partnership itself is not subject to tax.

Limited partnerships

In some states there are (already existing or moves to introduce) what is known as *limited partnerships*. These structures allow a partner to invest a certain amount of money into a partnership with the liability of that party being limited to the amount invested. The law (particularly that affecting taxation aspects) on limited partnerships has recently been changed, so consult your solicitor for further information on the latest situation in your state or territory.

Cross partnership agreements

One way of lessening the pressure on a partnership is to enter into a cross partnership arrangement. This can be a very effective alternative to a formal partnership. I call this a *'Claytons partnership'*. In other words; *it's the partnership you have when you're not having a partnership!*

This arrangement presents a way of still working together without the total sharing arrangements involved in a normal partnership agreement. The key to this arrangement is to break up the business into separate parts. Each party decides which part of the business he or she will be responsible for, and then each party does their own thing. This is then tied together with a legal agreement which binds each of them to the other person's business. In certain situations this can work very well. Many businesses can be effectively split into two or more separate entities.

For instance, let's say that two people wanted to set up a business making and selling clothing. One person is a tailor and the other a salesperson. Instead of forming a partnership and putting all their resources and finances together, they might consider two completely separate and independent businesses. One could be the XYZ Manufacturing Co and the other XYZ Sales Company. Each business would be responsible for its own expenses and profit or loss situation. The two parties involved could then draw up an agreement between themselves (through a solicitor) which may even say that XYZ Manufacturing can supply only XYZ Sales and XYZ Sales can buy only through XYZ Manufacturing.* In other words, neither can survive without the other. Both businesses are still independent but dependent on each other.

To protect themselves they could insert a proviso that if either party failed to supply the goods or services to an agreed price or standard, that business could have the right to sell to or buy from another source. It sounds complicated but it is really quite straightforward. You are simply breaking the business up into two separate profit centres. This is a common management practice in many large firms.

The beauty of this arrangement is you don't have all the usual problems associated with a partnership. If the owner of one company wants to take their spouse on an all-expenses paid business trip around the world, it comes out of his or her share of the profits from within *their* business.

Of course, the above arrangement will not work in every type of business situation but with the use of a little bit of lateral thinking, it can be made to work in most. Think about it, it could save you a lot of the heartaches that all too often accompany partnership arrangements.

Warning: Make sure you don't contravene any restrictive trade practices laws in relation to exclusive dealings.

7. THE FRANCHISE ALTERNATIVE

"Buying a franchise is a way of going into business for yourself but not by yourself. "
Anon.

Franchising has undergone rapid growth in recent times and it has been estimated that by the year 2000, over 50 per cent of all retail business turnover in this country will be generated by some sort of franchised outlet.

Generally speaking, the success rate of franchised businesses is far higher than that of non-franchised businesses. However, this does certainly not mean that all franchised businesses are good businesses. On the contrary, of the hundreds of systems on offer, only a relative few are real long term money making propositions and many are not worth the money. A number of franchised businesses have featured in the news recently for making promises to prospective franchisees about unrealistic returns and it is definitely a case of buyer beware. Any proposition should be approached with extreme caution. That said, let's have a look at some of the advantages and disadvantages of franchised businesses.

Exactly what is a franchised business?
The concept of franchising is relatively simple, and this is probably the major reason for its rapid growth. It involves taking a proven business concept or system and duplicating it in another place or area of the market. This is what is known as *business format franchising* and it first appeared in Australia in the early 1970s with the introduction of McDonalds and some other American fast food outlets.

Under a typical franchise system, the franchisor sells the rights to a business system and the use of the name to the franchisee for a fee. There is usually an ongoing charge known as a *royalty* or *management fee,* based on a percentage of sales turnover and an advertising levy for ongoing promotion and advertising.

Around half of all the franchise systems operating in Australia are business format franchises and the other half are petroleum industry franchised outlets. In the early days, most franchise concepts were for fast food but as the concept of franchising matures, we are seeing a much greater variety of industries being franchised. This now includes fields as diverse as industrial hose pipes and education, to suburban lawyers and graphic designers.

Major benefits

The major advantage of a franchise lies in buying a proven business concept with the full benefit of somebody else's experience and knowledge. You should also have this person's guidance, at least during the critical starting up time. Other advantages could include any or all of the following:

- *group promotion and bulk buying power*
- *less time to establish a positive cash flow*
- *exclusive territory, which limits the risk of competition*
- *a 'ready made' market*
- *savings on the purchase of plant and equipment*
- *the security of a reliable source of supply for product*
- *initial and ongoing training*
- *a good idea of how much capital is needed before you start out*
- *a strong element of recognition of the concept by the public through the use of a common image.*

A good franchisor will also usually undertake ongoing market research to determine trends and demands, hopefully leading to continual improvement and introduction of new products. This type of research can be very expensive and is not generally available to the independent business owner.

You also have the benefit of being able to talk to the other franchisees. Sharing ideas and experiences with other people with similar interests to you can help to overcome the feeling of loneliness experienced by many independent business operators.

Disadvantages

It is very important to stress that not all franchise concepts are safe, secure investments. Nor is it any sort of a guarantee of success for people who are lazy, incompetent, careless or just unsuited to running their own business. There have been some notable failures of franchise concepts in Australia. I know of several people who have bought franchises and lost heavily, in some cases through no fault of their own. Just as much care should be taken when buying into a franchise (perhaps even more where large amounts of money are involved).

One of the disadvantages of purchasing a franchise is you actually have very little control over your own destiny once you are locked into the system. If you are unfortunate enough to purchase a franchise from an unscrupulous or incompetent franchisor, you may well find yourself in a situation where you can do very little about it. Often you are locked into a location by a long lease and the franchisor controls the supply of goods and the advertising and promotion of them. If the goods are not up to scratch or the supply is unreliable, you could find yourself trapped between a rock and a hard place.

The following is a summary of some the possible disadvantages:

- *higher cost of entry into the franchise system*
- *loss of some independence and the need to follow exact procedures*
- *risk of the franchise system itself collapsing*
- *possible lack of ability to be able to expand into other areas*
- *risk that the franchise will become unprofitable*
- *possibility that the franchisor will include conditions in the franchise agreement which disadvantage the franchisee.*

While the profitability of a franchise might be comparable or even higher than that of an independent business, it is fair to say that most franchise concepts are not *'get-rich-quick'* schemes. Generally, they are more suitable for the person who wants to minimise the risk involved in setting up a business and is prepared to take the 'slow and steady' approach to starting their own business.

Note: In my experience there are not too many get-rich-quick small businesses of the non-franchise type either - certainly not legal ones anyway! Most of the people I know who have got rich from a small business, got that way by working hard over a long period of time.

Finance

Most of the major banks now have a franchise division, which specialises in financing franchisees. The competition between banks offering finance for franchisees is fairly severe and you will generally find them helpful. You are usually required to have about 30 to 40 per cent of the purchase price before seeking a loan, although this will vary depending on the bank, the type of franchise you are buying and the overall amount of capital required. Banks generally keep a list of 'acceptable' franchise concepts (ones they will readily lend money on). This is an added safeguard for you. They may not admit to the existence of such a list, nor tell you who is or is not on it but I would be very wary of borrowing money to purchase a franchise system if a bank advised against it for any reason at all.

It must be stressed however, that even if a bank does approve a loan on a franchised business it is no guarantee whatsoever that the concept is totally sound or fail-proof.

Summary

There is a lot to be said for having the full benefit of somebody else's hindsight and anyone considering going into business should at least explore and consider very carefully the franchise alternative. While the cost of entry might appear high, it may well be worth the expense to minimise the risk of failure, especially if you have no previous experience in running your own business.

8. WHICH FRANCHISE SHOULD YOU BUY?

"Choose a job you love and you will never have to work a day in your life."
Confucius

Should you decide to buy a franchised business, your next task will be to evaluate which system you are going to buy into. With over 400 to choose from, this can be an extremely difficult decision.

There are a number of factors you need to consider. Firstly, what type of business are you best suited to? With some franchise systems you need to have experience in a particular trade before they will accept you. This applies to such things as real estate, coaching, plumbing, etc; however the greatest percentage of business format franchises do not require any specialist experience and training is usually provided.

All good franchisors require their potential franchisees to go through a screening process, to make sure that they are 'suitable' to the system. During this screening process, the franchisor will generally be looking at your managerial skills and your temperament, as well as your financial capacity. They may also consider your people skills and your appearance, amongst other things. In some of the best franchises, this screening process is very intensive. In the case of one large, well-known franchise system, it said that there are over 100 applicants rejected for every one accepted! They obviously believe that there is a lot more to becoming a successful franchisee than simply being able to cook a hamburger!

In many ways, buying into a franchise is a bit like entering into a marriage agreement - it can only work out satisfactorily if the two parties are compatible. As with any business, you should consider whether the system fulfils your wants and needs. Are you looking for a satisfying and rewarding career or just simply a chance to earn big money? If you have enjoyed a challenging management career to date, are you going to be happy with simply putting a scoop of ice cream on the end of a cone or are you going to be looking for something which provides a greater challenge?

On the other hand, you may well be at the stage of your business career where you could be very happy with a less complicated life. I know of one high-ranking bank executive who bought an ice cream franchise and is very happy with his new career!

You should also give consideration to the type of lifestyle you want. There is not much point in buying a fast food outlet if you are not prepared to work on weekends and late at night. Don't kid yourself that you will be able to pay someone else to do this part of the job for you. You will probably find in reality that honest, reliable staff are hard to come by, and the responsibility will ultimately rest with you. Naturally, you should also consider the financial aspects and make sure that the system you are buying will be able to provide you with sufficient income to at least maintain your present lifestyle, if not improve it.

Professional advice

With so many franchise systems out there to choose from, you should be able to find something that suits. There are a number of organisations that can help you with your choice, including specialist franchise consultants who will give you advice for a fee. Be warned however, some consultants get a fee from the franchisor for finding suitable applicants, so the advice you receive may not be totally unbiased. If you do seek the advice of a consultant, ask at the outset if they receive any form of payment from franchisors.

There are also a number of legal firms that now have franchise consultancies as a part of their practice, as well as accountants who specialise in the area.

Before signing any agreement or documentation to purchase a franchise, make sure that you deal with an accountant and particularly a solicitor who specialises in franchising. The franchise department of your bank should be able to make recommendations in this area.

Another body that can be most helpful is the Franchisors Association of Australia & NZ (FAANZ). Check your local telephone book or ring their head office on (02) 9891 4933. This association, which has been in operation since 1982, is a self regulating body made up mainly of franchisors. In order to become a member of FAANZ, franchisors must satisfy certain operating conditions and must also abide by a code of ethics. FAANZ will supply you with a list of their members and I would recommend that you check with them before dealing with any franchise system to see if they are a registered member.

It must be stressed that membership of FAANZ does not give any sort of special guarantee of integrity or competence but it is another form of safeguard.

Evaluating a franchise system

So, how do you go about evaluating a franchise system? Firstly, you must assess whether you possess the skills required to successfully operate the business system you are considering or alternatively, that you can easily acquire them.

One of the best forms of checking out the claims of franchisors is to talk to as many of the other franchisees in the system as possible. Reputable franchisors will not mind you talking to their other members and most people will be happy to share their experiences with you. When talking to other franchisees in the system, don't just ask them if they are happy doing what they are doing. Ask them if the profits and sales performance are up to expectations and promises. Is the level of ongoing support, such as training, advertising and promotion satisfactory?

A word of warning; when you are approaching other franchisees, be mindful of that person's time. Don't walk in on them unannounced in the middle of their lunchtime rush hour and expect them to drop everything and start talking to you. Remember, they are trying to run a business.

Check out the credentials of the franchisor with a fine tooth comb. This includes getting a mercantile report from a credit service agency such as Dun & Bradstreet. Ask your bank to assist you in checking out their bona fides. Check with the Department of Fair Trading to see if any litigation has been brought down against the system operators.

Make sure that the industry you are joining is well established and the product or service being offered is not just a short-term fad that is likely to eventually go out of fashion. Check out how many outlets are in operation and how long they have been going. How many of the outlets are owned and operated by the franchisors themselves? Generally speaking, the more they own themselves the better. Have they experienced strong, steady growth or have they simply mushroomed up overnight? Have they ever terminated any of their franchisees and if so, what were the reasons? What is the background and experience level of the people operating the franchise system? What level of support and ongoing training are they offering? Ask to meet the person or persons you will be dealing with after you have bought the system. This is important, as you will probably have to work closely with that person in the future. It is always easier to deal with a person whom you like and trust. Ask the franchisor if you can work for a short time in one of the outlets (without pay) just to get a feel of what the business is all about. If the franchisor starts ducking and weaving at this request, I would start looking for another franchise.

The agreement

At the heart of any good franchise system is a good franchise agreement. While it is likely to be a long and detailed document, it should be written in plain English and be easy to understand. *Naturally, do not even think about signing any agreement without seeing your solicitor first!* However, before you do this you should be reasonably clear of just what your obligations are going to be and also the obligations of the franchisor.

There are many aspects that you need to consider including the following:

- *What are the terms of terminating the contract if you decide to sell?*
- *What is the duration of the agreement and what are the terms of renewal?*

58

- *Is there a renewal fee?*
- *Will you be paid for any goodwill you create, should you decide to sell the business later?*
- *Can you easily sell the business if you decide you don't like it?*
- *If you are buying a geographical territory, make sure it is clearly defined and that other people can't open up in the same business too close to you.*

Note, this last point is very important. A friend of mine purchased an outlet in a Sydney suburb for a very large, well-known franchise system with a world-wide reputation. Due to the enthusiasm of an over zealous franchise salesman here, within a very short space of time they opened 12 outlets in the Sydney metropolitan area. He later discovered that this same system had only two outlets for the whole of San Francisco! He soon discovered the local market was hopelessly over-catered for and eventually he had to get out, losing a good deal of money. Check how many outlets the company is intending to open and make sure the market demand is adequate.

Summary
Take your time in assessing any franchise system; it doesn't matter if this means six months or even longer. It is quite common for people to take this long to properly evaluate a franchise. Remember, if you make the wrong choice you will have a long time to think about your regrets. Be very wary of franchisors whose major concern seems to be getting your signature on the dotted line and/or your deposit cheque. Good franchisors will be just as concerned about you as you are about them (or even more so). A failed franchisee is bad for their reputation in the long term.

And finally, don't fall in love with the idea of the concept and forget to do your homework properly.

9. THE SEVEN STEPS

"If you could get up the courage to begin, you have the courage to succeed."
David Viscott

There are many things that need to be considered before you enter into a business of your own and a great deal of preparation is required. Here is a short list of the seven basic steps that you need to follow to get you underway:

Step 1: Are you suited?
The first and most crucial step you must take is to decide whether or not you are suited to running your own business. While most people like the idea of working for themselves and the independence of being their own boss, not everybody has the right temperament to run their own business. Some people are much better off working for somebody else. Make sure you have the right mental attitude to succeed. Think long and hard about what is involved. Make sure you are prepared to give it your all. Success and dedication are required and it is never going to be an easy ride, so make sure you have what it takes. Talk to other people in business and make certain you understand fully what you are letting yourself in for.

Step 2: Which type of business?
If you do decide you are suited, your next step is to determine which type of business you are going to enter. You should give a lot of thought to this, after all, you are probably going to spend a lot of your time doing it and you may also be risking a good deal of

money, time and effort. Your chances of succeeding are much higher if you choose a business that you like and one that is suited to your area of expertise. In making this decision, you should take into account the following points:

- *Is it a growing industry.?*
- *How will your competitors react to your entry into the market?*
- *What advantages (if any) do you have over your competitors?*
- *Can you compete on price? If you are relying on price, what is your leverage?*
- *Are your competitors likely to try and price you out of the market? Can you offer better service or greater expertise?*
- *Should you buy an established business or start up yourself from scratch? (There are advantages both ways).*
- *Would you be better off joining a good franchise system? Your chances of success could be greatly increased if you buy a franchise (see Franchising chapters).*

The various state and territory government small business agencies can be of great assistance. Most of them run short courses in starting and running a business and they have large amounts of literature available, often at no charge.

Step 3: What are your strengths?
The next step is to do an audit of your skills and capabilities. Do you possess the necessary expertise to conduct the business yourself or will you be relying on other people? If you are going to learn new skills, is the training offered adequate? Does the business chosen suit your personality and lifestyle requirements? Take an honest look at your attitude and ability to work.

Step 4: Your financial position
Next, examine your financial position closely. Establish how much money you will require to finance your business. In calculating the amount needed, take into account working capital and wages for yourself and any staff, not forgetting such things as workers' compensation, payroll tax, compulsory superannuation and other on-costs.

Your industry association or the Department of Industrial

Relations should be able to tell you about relevant awards, or talk to your state or territory government small business agency.

What finance do you have available, what sort of a loan do you need, and what assets do you have that can be used as security for a loan? There is an old adage that says once you have calculated the amount you need to start up you should then double it! This might be a little bit excessive but make sure you build in a buffer. You should also decide where you are going to run your business from. Can it be run from home or will you need to rent or buy premises?

Step 5: Planning
The next step is to start drawing up your business plan. After you have completed it, take it along to your accountant and get him or her to go over the figures with you to determine whether your plan is viable. Your accountant can also advise you on which accounting methods and bookkeeping systems you should employ, to ensure that your business is on the right course. If you monitor your turnover, profit margin and finances right from the start you will greatly increase your chances of success.

If you are going to buy an existing business or a franchise system, you will need an assessment of the worth of the business and its ongoing ability to make money. Your accountant should be able to tell you whether the price quoted is fair and whether the figures presented are realistic. Try to get an accountant with extensive experience and other clients in your chosen industry. Your accountant will be able to tell you if your projections are realistic and achievable.

Step 6: The structure
The next person to see is your solicitor. If you are buying an existing business or franchise system, they will need to look at the contract to make sure you are fully protected. Your solicitor (probably in consultation with your accountant) will be able to advise which business structure you should use (sole trader, partnership, company or trust). They will also be able to help you with such things as registering your business name and any trade marks or other details.

Step 7: The bank

The final step (especially if your business venture is going to require finance) is to consult your bank. Many people make the mistake of going to see the bank first. But if you do your homework beforehand, the bank won't ask you questions that you don't know the answers to. By the time you get to the bank, you should have prepared a sound business plan and have a concise idea of exactly how much money you will require. And by making a professional presentation, your application for finance will have a much greater chance of success.

10. THE THREE WISE MEN

*(or women)**

"To survive and prosper in business you need three accomplices: a good accountant, a good solicitor and a good bank manager."
Anon.

This advice is as true today as it ever was, but where do you find these three wise people? *(And yes, there are an ever increasing number of women appearing in all of these professions but to save driving us both crazy with the him/her business, I will take the liberty of using the term 'him' in the generic sense here, just for this chapter, I promise!)*
Let's deal with them one at a time:

Choosing an accountant
John Cornell (Paul Hogan's good mate and manager), is perhaps not somebody who immediately springs to mind as your typical business guru. However, in an interview I once read about his business affairs, he made the following very astute observation:
"Years ago, if you were in business, you used to hire a part-time bookkeeper to come into your office for half a day a week at a cost of around $50 a time. This was your entire expenditure on accountancy. Now, your accountant probably charges $250 an hour and you go and visit him. Furthermore, he is probably located on the top floor of a luxury downtown office block with sweeping views and original oil paintings on the walls!" For a bloke that always played the part of a moron, that was a pretty perceptive observation from old Strop!
They were the good old days - what happened?

Unfortunately the laws of this country, particularly those relating to taxation, are generally made by solicitors or ex-solicitors. It has been estimated that around 35 per cent of our politicians are ex-legal people and they love to keep their mates in work. So, the system just continues to get more and more complex and we are probably stuck with it for the foreseeable future.

Getting the right advice can make a difference of thousands of dollars to your bottom line or could even affect your very survival, so it is vitally important to get an accountant that's right for you. Some accountants seem to adopt the attitude that they are working for the taxation office (not you) and that it is their duty to see that you pay the maximum amount of tax possible. While it is their legal duty to make sure you pay the *correct* amount of tax, you certainly don't need someone who is going to create ways for you to pay more than you have to!

Let's get one thing very straight and clear right here and now: *I am not for one moment suggesting that you should try to get out of paying any tax that you legally owe or that you should even consider paying less than your fair share.* I am simply saying that if you can avoid paying more tax than you have to, then you should. That is your right in a free country. Tax avoidance is quite legal, tax evasion on the other hand is not and there are some very stiff penalties, including large fines and prison sentences if you are caught engaging in the latter.

Be warned: Accountants who will tell you of ways to cheat the system are a dying breed!

A number of laws have been passed in recent years that make accountants personally liable, if they advise you to take illegal actions to evade taxation. Consequently, not many of them these days are foolish enough or gung ho enough to take the chance. Also, even if you are simply acting on the advice given by them, if it is not legal you will still be personally liable and have to face the consequences.

A good accountant, of course, is not there just to show you ways of minimising your tax. He can also assist you with developing your business and advise on business decisions. A good accountant can become your personal business mentor. Unfortunately, even though accountants today are trained in all sorts of skills to assist you in your business, only a relatively small number of them become involved in services outside the traditional accountancy role.

During my many years in business, I have had several accountants and it is probably fair to say that, like the curate's egg, all of them were good in parts. And not unexpectedly, all of them had some shortcomings. Business and taxation law is now so complex it is unfair to expect one person to know it all and more and more solicitors are getting into the act. A good mate of mine who gives advice in financial planning, says that you should hire the *best* tax solicitor you can find and the *cheapest* accountant. I can't tell you if it works or not but it is an interesting theory and incidentally, he is now a multi-millionaire!

Of course, the best legal advice available doesn't come cheaply and there are two problems with this:

(a) you probably can't afford it;
(b) you probably don't need it; at least not in the early part of your business life.

It may make good sense for a high flying entrepreneur who is earning $10,000 a week (assuming that there are still such people in existence) to seek the best taxation advice available. And if your accountant is able to save you $1,000,000 in tax, then you probably won't mind paying him $200,000 for his services. However, if you are not quite in this league yet, you are going to have to settle for someone a little bit down the line.

In making your selection, the first question you should ask yourself is, *"What do I expect of my accountant?"* Do you have a major tax problem? Are you earning megabucks and need to set yourself up in an offshore tax haven or are you just looking for some sound, sensible advice on taxation and record keeping?

Important note: It should also be pointed out here that there is a difference between an accountant and a bookkeeper. Most small business starters have a tendency to confuse the two functions. Generally, you will not use your accountant to keep your books for you on a day-to-day basis. Bookkeeping or record keeping, is a separate job from the normal duties of your accountant. The average accountant charges far too much on an hourly rate to do general bookkeeping. Although some accountancy firms do offer bookkeeping as an additional service, the best and cheapest way is usually to do it yourself or get a family member to do it for you.

If the bookkeeping side of your business gets too much for you, there are a large number of professional bookkeeping services available in most areas. Generally their prices are reasonable and their services are quick and efficient. If you have a really large number of transactions every month, it may pay you to put in a computer. However, you may still find it is cheaper and easier to use the services of a computer bureau, at least initially. Unless you are highly skilled in computer operation, you may well find that the time required to learn how to operate the computer is better spent developing other areas of your business.

The selection process

Once you have sorted out the question of exactly what it is you require of your accountant, you must then go through the process of finding one who is right for you. Accountants are just like any other segment of the community, they come in a variety of types. There are conservative accountants, creative accountants, caring accountants and gung ho accountants. There are expensive ones, cheap ones, efficient ones and inefficient ones. Your task is to find the one who best suits your needs at the time.

It is important to bear this in mind, because it is possible to *outgrow* your accountant, just like your premises or other equipment in your business. That might sound a bit cold blooded and maybe your accountant is one of those who is going to grow with you. Your accountant may become your close friend and confidant over the years and you may wish to stick with the same one, regardless. And by the way, this can happen in reverse, I once had an accountant who outgrew me! He got swallowed up as part of a big firm who only wanted to deal with big clients and he immediately doubled my bill.

Don't be afraid to change if you are unhappy with the service you are getting from your accountant or you feel you can find somebody else who will offer you a better deal. I have often heard people bemoaning the inefficiency or even the charges of their accountant but then adding, "I should make a change but he's been doing my books for years, etc." Don't fall into this trap. Always have an open mind and be receptive to offers of a better deal or a better service.

This brings up another point - don't be frightened to query your accountant's (or solicitor's) bill, if you feel it is unjustified or over the top. Some professional people are not opposed to charging like wounded bulls, especially if they think they can get away with it. There are unscrupulous operators out there who will send you a ridiculously high bill and then drop it by quite a large amount if you query it. They work on the theory that most people grudgingly pay up and are too timid to challenge it. *It's called the run-the-flag-up the-flagpole-and-see-if-they-salute-it method.*

These types may be in the minority but they do exist and you should be ever vigilant in trying to avoid being ripped off. I once protested loudly to my accountant about his bill and pointed out it was about 40 per cent more than he had charged me for the previous year, way ahead of inflation. I also suggested that he had not really done much more work in that year than the previous one. I was pleasantly surprised to see the bill reduced by several hundred dollars. *Not a bad result for the cost of a telephone call and a bit of moaning and groaning!* This experience also taught me a valuable lesson - never pay a bill if you feel it is not right or too expensive, always query it.

Summary
Choose your accountant carefully. Get someone who is familiar with your industry. Ask him what other clients he has in your line of trade. Ask other people in the trade for recommendations. Don't be afraid to ask him up front what his fees are likely to be. It's no good having an accountant who you are too frightened to say *'hello'* to in case he sends you a bill!

Above all, get somebody that you feel comfortable with. You should be able to talk to your accountant in the same way as you would talk to your mates down at the local pub. You should not feel in any way intimidated by his superior knowledge; after all, you are paying his bill and he is working for you. *That doesn't mean to say that you should be arrogant either.* Treat your accountant with the same respect and courtesy you would like to be treated with yourself. Find somebody you can work with and you feel comfortable with. Someone you respect, trust and can confide in.

Wherever possible, involve your accountant in the important decisions of your business. Don't just go and see him once a year at tax time, after all the damage has been done. Even if you don't take his advice, you will at least have somebody there to play devil's advocate and point out any pitfalls.

Choosing a solicitor

Be warned: Many solicitors genuinely believe that money grows on trees and that you have one of these trees growing in your backyard!

They can be and usually are, outrageously expensive. Of course, they are a necessary part of doing business and you won't go far without them. They can also save you or make you thousands of dollars by giving you the right advice.

These days, the law is so specialised you will probably need more than one solicitor during your business life. The tricky part lies in knowing when you have to use them and when you can do without them. This doesn't mean that you should always try and do your own thing, this can be disastrous. It simply means that if you *can* resolve a matter without resorting to the courts, then do so.

Before you consult your lawyer, have a good idea of what you want him to do for you. If at all possible, draft up a rough of any agreements, etc. to save time. Remember, with these people - time really is money!

For straightforward legal matters (like signing a lease on premises) a good suburban solicitor in a small practice is fine and he will generally charge you a lot less than his big practice counterpart. He may also give you better service on relatively mundane matters which are subject to a scale of charges and may be looked on as something of a nuisance to a big firm.

Make sure your solicitor has other clients involved in your industry. You may be surprised at how important this can be. A solicitor involved in your industry can be a big help to you in other ways, apart from just legal matters. A good solicitor with his ear to the

69

ground can supply you with information about what is happening in your industry and point out opportunities.

Finally, in choosing your general solicitor, as in the case of the accountant, you should find somebody that you can talk to on an equal basis. Don't put up with mumbo jumbo or legalese. Make sure that you have a reasonably good understanding of what is going on in any legal matters. Don't just blindly put yourself in their hands.

I'm not suggesting that you become a *'Perry Mason'* but a good working knowledge of business law will be a big help during your business career. And you will be surprised at what you can pick up by listening intently and reading books and articles in business magazines on the subject.

Choosing your bank manager

Last but not least, there is the elusive so called *'good bank manager.'* Where on earth do you find one of these when you need one?

Unfortunately, 'good' bank managers aren't as easy to find as they used to be. Changes in the banking industry and changing attitudes have seen to that. Indeed, some banks now have a system where if you ring up to apply for a loan, you are directly transferred to a head office loans department. The banks would argue that this new system is better than the old system (where you developed a close working relationship with your local bank manager) because you are dealing with a 'loans' specialist. However, this tends to depersonalise the system and everybody is treated as a number in the computer rather than a person.

Some banks still do give their individual managers a certain amount of leeway to negotiate, particularly when it comes to overdraft limits, the most popular form of funding working capital for small businesses. Unfortunately, this leeway has been curtailed dramatically of late due largely to the activities of the high flying entrepreneurs of the 1980s.

As to which bank has the best system and which bank has the best bank managers, it's difficult to say. I have heard stories from business owners of poor treatment by the manager of a certain bank and then a short time later, someone else will tell me they have a terrific bank manager with a different branch of the same bank. Of course, a lot depends on the customer's attitude and how honest he or she has been with the manager in the first place. It is amazing how many people make no arrangement with the bank or fail to keep their manager informed about the conditions in their business and then get terribly upset when the bank bounces a cheque on them because they went over their limit. You should always keep your manager advised if you look like going over your limit. Bank managers hate nasty little surprises and can quickly lose their sense of humour in such cases.

The bank manger and lunch

When talking to small business owners, the following two questions often arise:

"Should I take the bank manager to lunch?" and *"Will it help?"*

The answer to the first question is, *"yes"* and the second, *"probably, under some circumstances"*. You should try to develop a good working relationship with your bank manager. This doesn't mean that you have to have him over to your house for dinner every night or that you should name your first born child after him, although this could help. *(Joking, of course!)*

The best way to keep your bank manager on side is to keep him informed about what is happening in your business. It is a good idea to invite him to come and have a look at your operation so he can better understand it. This may also be a good time to invite him to lunch. The ideal situation would be to invite him to come and have a look at what you're doing and then have lunch afterwards. This should be a friendly, getting-to-know-you exercise.

Warning: Never discuss heavy financial problems or ask your bank manager for a loan or an extension of your overdraft limit over lunch!

This will probably only serve to give him severe heartburn and get you offside with him forever. Save your discussions of detailed financial matters for the office. The lunch should be relaxed, friendly and in a non-threatening environment.

Summary

Finding a good bank manager you can work with can sometimes be a case of trial and error. Recommendations from other business people can be very helpful, especially if the person is well known to the manager and is prepared to take you in and personally introduce you.

Here's a tip: If it's at all convenient, try to bank with a large, busy branch (you can always have signatures at a more convenient smaller branch location for day-to-day transactions). The reason for this is, banks tend to give their big branch managers a much bigger discretionary limit (the amount the manager can approve at his own discretion before he has to refer to head office). However; if you are a very small business this may not be so helpful because in a large branch, you could find yourself dealing with the accountant or even the assistant accountant if your account is relatively small.

Finally, don't lose sight of the fact in all of this that any money you borrow from a bank has to be paid back!

Borrowing money can be very expensive. Try to limit the amount you use by collecting your outstanding debts on time and minimising your stock holdings. I have seen lots of people take out bigger and bigger overdrafts, simply to fund their debtors' businesses rather than their own! Don't increase your overdraft and then get lazy about collecting money owed to you. Remember, the lower your overdraft is, the more profitable your business will be and the more money you will be able to put in your own pocket.

11. HOME BASE OR PREMISES?

"Even if you're on the right track, you'll get run over if you just sit there."
Will Rogers

One of the more popular alternatives for new business startups, is to work from home. It is estimated that over 250,000 people in Australia currently run businesses from a home base. This is highly recommended (if at all practical) because it is obviously cheaper and avoids the need for you to sign a long lease on premises. Starting out from home is also a good way of *'testing the water'* before plunging into the deep end. Many a small business has failed leaving the proprietors stuck with a long lease (usually backed by personal guarantees) that has to be paid.

It must be stressed however, that there are limitations to operating a business from home and several factors need to be considered. Is your business suited to operating from a home base? Is the layout, design and location of the home suitable? Is there enough room to carry on the business without disrupting the family routine too much? Are you likely to run into problems with local council because the zoning is strictly residential and are you likely to get complaints from neighbours about pollution, noise or other disturbances?

If you can overcome these problems, there are a number of other benefits to be gained by operating from a home base. For starters, there is the saving in travelling time to and from the workplace and the ability to be able to work at any hour of the day or night when necessary. Of course, this can also be a trap. When the work has piled up, it is sometimes difficult when you are running a home-based business to avoid the temptation of spending every spare moment you have in the business.

Self discipline

You must also decide if you are the type of person who is easily self-motivated. Many people thrive on their daily contact with other people outside the home and working from home can be a very lonely experience. There is always a danger of becoming introverted and depressed. You will also need a high degree of self discipline. Even though when you are working from home you may be able to vary your hours from the normal working hours, I don't recommend it. I worked from home for a number of years and found it imperative to maintain a strict time schedule. I would shower, shave and dress for work in the normal way, making sure I was at my desk before 9am every morning. It is very important to establish a working routine.

A friend of mine who runs a training business from home, tells me she gets up every morning and dresses as if she were going to the office. She then gets into her car and drives around the block, arriving back at the house ready for work! She finds this exercise necessary to get her mind into the *'work mode.'* As silly as this may sound, if you have trouble starting in the mornings you should give it a try. You might be surprised at how well it works for you.

When working from a home base, it is essential also to establish your work routine with the rest of the family right from the outset. Sit down with your spouse and children and spell out your timetable. When you are working they should consider that you have literally *'gone to work'* and are not able to be interrupted with noise or other distractions. Establish a solid routine and let them know that you will be having morning tea and lunch at a certain time. This way if they need to talk to you about non-business matters, they can do so at these allotted times, rather than continually interrupting your work flow.

Expenses attached to running a business from home are generally tax deductible. This includes such items as part of the electricity and telephone bills. To substantiate these claims however, you will need to satisfy the taxation office that a certain part of the home has been set aside strictly for business. So far as the home itself is concerned, you should be able to claim a part of your mortgage repayments as a legitimate business expense. *Be warned however, if you do take this course of action you could lose part of the tax free capital gain on your home, should you decide to sell it later on.* Also, a number of what appeared to be straightforward legitimate claims for home office expenses have been rejected by the taxation department. You may find the loss of the tax free capital gain and substantiating a claim are just not worth the hassle for the small concession allowed. Speak to your accountant about this before taking action.

Maintaining your image

If you do decide to work from home, it is important to maintain a professional image at all times. This is particularly important when it comes to answering the telephone. Make sure incoming calls are answered in a professional manner, even though you might be the only person answering the telephone. It sounds much more professional to answer the phone in the name of the business. For instance, *"Good morning, XYZ Importing, Fred Smith speaking"*, sounds a lot better than a simple *"Hello"*.

Avoid having children answering the phone or domestic background noises such as washing machines going or dogs barking. It may pay you to consider putting in a second telephone line which is used strictly for business. If your business takes you out of the home during normal business hours, give some serious consideration to having a mobile telephone or at least a car phone. You will probably find the extra business gained makes the added expense well worthwhile.

If it is not always possible to answer the phone yourself, you can have your incoming calls diverted to another number or even your mobile phone. You could also have them diverted to an answering service, so that the phone is still answered in your own name and messages taken. If you are going to be out of the home office most of the time and you don't have somebody there who can answer your calls in a businesslike manner, consider using an answering service and ringing in periodically to get your messages.

While it costs a little extra, use a service that answers in *your name*, not a telephone number that is used by numerous businesses. There is some very sophisticated communication equipment avail-

76

able these days, including pocket pagers that bleep you and give you your written messages, electronic mail boxes and much, much more. Discuss the options with your local telephone sales office. Good communications are a vital part of your business and can make a tremendous difference to your bottom line. Whether you work from home or from outside premises, don't miss business through being difficult to contact.

The serviced office option

If you are in a situation where you either can't operate from home or don't want to and yet still don't feel confident enough to sign a long lease on business premises, there is another option, the *serviced office*.

Serviced offices are an excellent alternative for the small business operator. There are now a large number of these centres in most capital cities and major regional centres. Usually they provide immediate occupancy of a fully furnished office, complete with telephone answering and secretarial services on an ad hoc basis. This often includes word processing, reception, typing, photocopying, telex, fax, mail, courier service, boardroom and kitchen facilities.

The great thing about these centres is that you have all the modern conveniences of a well-equipped office at your fingertips without the capital outlay for expensive items like fax machines and photocopiers. At the same time, you only pay for these services as and when you use them. Some serviced offices come with storage space in the industrial areas or sweeping views from the top floor of a prestigious building in the heart of the central business district. One in the heart of the Sydney CBD even boasts an indoor swimming pool and gym and some also offer the use of office facilities interstate and overseas.

Another advantage of the serviced office is, if you find that your business outgrows the space, you can simply rent more. Usually there is no long-term lease and most of them operate on a monthly rental basis. If you need to use a boardroom or conference room, this is available on an hourly charge. Many companies pay big rentals for boardrooms that sit idle for 80 to 90 per cent of the time.

Summary

As with most things in life, you only get what you pay for. Before paying top money for a luxurious, prestige location, carefully evaluate how many clients will actually be coming to see you (rather than you going to visit them). And remember, there is always the risk that if you look too far up-market, your clients may think you are charging too much! This will depend a lot on the industry you are in and the image you need to project. Take a good look around at the sort of premises your competitors are operating from and use this as a guide.

Look in your local Yellow Pages telephone directory or the classified section of your daily newspapers under the *'business premises to let'* section and check out the alternatives.

If you can possibly manage it, try working from home, at least in the early stages. Alternatively, a good, well-run serviced office presents a very viable and cost effective compromise between working from home and signing up for a long lease on business premises. And there is the added benefit of having other small business operators around you and even the possibility of doing reciprocal business with them or their network of associates.

12. LEASING PREMISES

*"There are some men who in a fifty-fifty proposition,
insist on getting the hyphen too."*
Lawrence J. Peter

Should you decide to operate your business from leased premises, you are going to have to face the daunting prospect of signing a lease. Leases are a minefield for the unwary. They contain delayed action mines that can go off six months, one year or three years later, usually when your business is facing its darkest hour. The best way to overcome these problems is to tackle them right from the outset. Tony Butcher of Brennans Solicitors in Mosman, Sydney has specialised in small business for a number of years and offers the following advice for successfully negotiating a lease:

Remember – *there is no such thing as a standard lease.* There is, however, a fairly standard procedure, which you may not like but you will be forced to accept. This standard procedure is put into motion once you have agreed to the lease offered. The lessor's solicitors will provide a lengthy document – sometimes 30 pages or more – which invariably contains clauses that were not discussed. *If they had been discussed, you would not have agreed to them!*

To add to this, the lessor's lawyers will insist that no amendments be made to the lease. The willingness to negotiate the terms will generally depend upon the desirability of the premises. It also used to be the case that the lessee had to pay the lessor's legal costs however, it is now becoming more common for the lessor to bear a proportion of their own legal costs.

Why is the lease of your business so important?

The lease document only ever becomes important if there is a dispute between lessor and lessee. Unfortunately, this is all too common. If you have an argument over the rent review or repairs, you will rush to your copy of the lease. If you have not taken care in negotiating the lease, you will find that the lessor has you *'over a barrel'*. The secret is to know what to ask for when negotiating a lease, what to look for when reviewing a lease and to agree on the important terms at the negotiation stage, so that the discretion of the lessor is limited.

Here is a useful guide to successfully negotiating a lease:

1. Keep it simple

Try to ensure the lessor's solicitor is using a Law Society approved precedent. Most states have approved precedents which are 'fairly' balanced.

2. Subletting and assignment

You may want to cover part of the rent by taking in tenants. If you don't specify this, the lease may exclude your right to do so.

3. Rent

Most people concentrate on getting a good deal with their rent. What they don't appreciate is that the rent will increase each year, sometimes staggeringly so. There are two types of review – the Consumer Price Index (CPI), which keeps up with inflation, and the market review, which brings the rent into line with other rental values. This can be a killer, because it means that even if your rent is particularly reasonable in the first year, a subsequent market review would destroy the benefit. Expect a CPI review every year, but try to avoid market reviews. Only agree to them every two or three years at most. Also, try to think ahead. If your premises are in an area where rents are destined to increase over the longer term, or say, when a specific development is completed, try to arrange it so that the revue is done before the development is completed.

4. Guarantees

If you are taking the lease in the name of your company, they will want personal guarantees, usually by the directors of the company. This is a good reason for not having your spouse involved in the company, especially if he or she is not playing an active role. Remember, you can now have companies with only one share holder and director.

5. Deposit

This is usually three month's rent and is kept by the lessor without interest. See if the lessor will agree to a bank guarantee instead. This simply involves the bank guaranteeing the amount without you actually having to pay out the money. There is a modest fee from the bank for this service but it is usually minimal and avoids your tying up money unnecessarily, which will help to preserve your precious working capital. If you can't get a bank guarantee, ensure the bond is kept in a real estate agent's trust account and is not just taken by the vendor.

6. Repairs

You would probably expect the lessor to be responsible but that's not always the case. Check it out.

7. Put the agreement in writing

The estate agent should do this for you. If not, set out the agreement using the above headings. Mark any correspondence, *'Subject to lease.'* Try to keep diary notes of any conversations you have with the real estate agents.

8. Rental term

Remember, you are committing yourself to a particular term. If your business doesn't succeed and you want to get out or if it does succeed and you need more or better space, you are still committed to the term of the lease.

Points to note:

Instruct a solicitor

Represent yourself on a murder trial or do your own conveyancing if you must but do not enter into a lease without your lawyer reviewing it. Any small business person who thinks they can do without the services of a lawyer when entering into a lease had better have a very good lawyer reviewing it - *they are going to need one!*

Read it

You don't have to tell me that legal documents are dull and written in a difficult manner. I know – I have to read them for a living! I appreciate there is so much small print nowadays, in everything from car lease agreements to credit card agreements. A lease you must read, however. Your lawyer will usually send you the lease with a covering letter. Sit down with a pencil and go through it, paragraph by paragraph. Make a note in the margin of any point you do not understand or are unhappy about and discuss it with your lawyer.

Insurance

A lease usually requires you to take out insurance. The clauses which deal with insurance are lengthy and may occur in three different places in the lease. Don't try to understand it. Just photocopy the relevant pages and send them to your insurance brokers. It will then be their problem. If you don't have an insurance broker, get your solicitor to recommend one.

Outgoings

These are usually included but if not, get details of them in writing. Some leases have complicated outgoings provisions. Make sure that the real estate agent has given you an estimate of the outgoings.

Demolition/renovation clauses

In my mind, this usually spells trouble and is to be avoided. If the lessor is renovating the premises or plans to knock them down, forget it and find something else. You may find yourself surrounded with dust and building works and with a lessor who expects to get your rent, while you have to carry on business on a building site!

Option to renew

Leases are often for three years, with an option to renew for a further three years. The lease will provide that you must give notice three months before expiry. If you don't do this, you will lose your option and your right to the premises. Make a note in your diary or somewhere you won't forget to take up your option.

Use

The lease will limit your use of the premises to certain activities. Make sure it covers your needs.

Assignment

Make sure that you can transfer the lease to someone else, should you find it necessary to vacate the premises before the lease expires.

Look around

Remember to exhaustively look around for the right premises. Visit the premises several times, ask other tenants what the landlord is like and whether the landlord maintains the building properly.

Summary

Getting a lease is one thing, living with it is another. It's a bit like like playing leapfrog with a unicorn. You've got to keep on your toes. Get it wrong and you are in big trouble!

Tony Butcher is a solicitor specialising in small business matters. Contact: (02) 9968 3800.

13. LOCAL GOVERNMENT

"If you are going to sin, sin against God, not the bureaucracy;
God will forgive you, the bureaucracy won't."
Hyman G. Rickover

People starting a business for the first time generally consider state and federal government requirements and go to great lengths to make sure they have all the appropriate licences but often forget all about the local council, usually at their peril.

Controls exercised by local government can be quite onerous and should never be disregarded or overlooked. This applies particularly to the use of premises or land for business purposes. Business activities started without local council approval can even be closed down by the council. This could be after you have spent considerable time, money and effort in starting up, promoting and generally developing your venture. Local governments in all states of Australia not only exercise considerable controls over the land and premises of businesses but also the means by which businesses identify and advertise themselves.

A good friend of mine, Pat Campbell, is a Sydney-based solicitor specialising in local government. He offers the following advice using typical scenarios of businesses that have ignored council requirements and warns of the implications:

Case one:
Fred Jones pays $45,000 plus stock at valuation for a small shop in a residential area. He either doesn't think about council or believes that there should be no problem, as the shop has been in existence for some time. Six months after he has taken over the business, a planning officer from the local council arrives and questions him about the shop. The officer points out that the land is zoned

residential and commercial activities are prohibited. Subsequently, Jones receives a notice from the council requiring him to stop trading as he is contravening the planning laws.

Case two:
Smith & Co. wishes to establish a warehouse and offices near the central business district. The leasing agent shows them a property and points out that other warehousing activities are occurring in the area. They commence operations and some time later the local council inspector arrives and asks if they have development consent to use the premises as a warehouse. Of course, they had not thought to go to the council. They subsequently receive a notice from council requiring them to lodge a development application and threatening legal proceedings to prevent the business continuing if they do not comply with the notice.

The above situations are typical and happen all too regularly. Imagine the shock of a proprietor of a business being threatened with closure, particularly where he or she has paid a lot of money for the given location and worked hard to establish the business. The difference between the two case studies above is:

- in Jones' case, the zoning prohibits his shop from operating;
- in Smith & Co's case, the zoning permits the activity only with the consent of the council. That is, it is only illegal while no development consent exists.

Jones could have severe legal problems and may lose his entire investment. If he bought a business which has been operating for many years, he may be able to claim that he can continue to operate contrary to the zoning. However, this depends on certain legal principles and facts to support them. It doesn't follow that because a business has been operating in the past, this gives it any legitimacy in terms of zoning or planning laws. (The law relating to 'existing use' is a separate and complex subject in itself.) It is important to also bear in mind that zoning laws change from time to time.
Smith & Co can apply to the council for development approval and they may be lucky enough to get it, but it does not necessarily follow that consent will be granted. There may be planning reasons

why council will refuse the application. Whatever the circumstances, it is more than likely that in order to protect the business, expensive and time-consuming legal proceedings may be required.

Development and building approvals
In general terms, all states contain town planning and local government legislation which require that in order to use land or buildings for particular activities, council grants a development consent, depending on how the land is zoned. Also, before altering or erecting a new building, a building approval must generally be obtained. This is distinct and separate from the development approval. Without either approval being granted, the council may be entitled to seek to have the business closed until it is regularised by a proper application and approval. In cases where an approval cannot be given (because it is contrary to zoning or the council is not prepared to approve it for planning or building reasons), the applicant is forced into legal conflict unless he or she accepts the decision of the council and walks away from the premises.

The only safe way to approach the purchase of a business or taking of a lease to establish a business is to ensure, prior to making a commitment (either by payment of purchase money, exchange of contracts or entry into a lease), that the necessary development and building approvals have been given for the building and its use. If you propose to use an existing building in a manner different from the way in which it was previously used or differently from the use permitted by zoning, you should apply to the council for a consent.

If you fail to obtain a development consent before commencing operations and the council is successful in preventing you from operating from the premises, you are likely to be at real risk under your lease. Most commercial leases now require tenants to obtain the necessary statutory approvals for their businesses, including council approvals. If you fail to obtain approval and are unable to operate from the premises, you may still be obliged under the lease to pay rent until such times as the premises are re-let.

It is generally naive and commercially unsound to believe that the landlord will play any role in ensuring that the premises can be used for the type of business you wish to establish. The tenant/business person cannot complain that the owner should have told them.

86

The landlord is generally not responsible for any failure to obtain approvals, although in certain circumstances it may be possible for you to sue the vendor, leasing agents or landowner for false statements as to how the building could be used. This is, however, a legal remedy which would involve expense and inconvenience and this is the last thing business people need, particularly in their formative years.

Advertising

Advertising is another area where businesses can fall foul of local government. Most businesses will want to *'hang out their shingle'* to identify the existence of their services and products. This usually takes the form of signage, either electronic or simply painted on the wall of the premises. Outdoor advertising and is usually controlled by local government and signs require approval.

This means that if you paint the wall of a building with your business name and detail some of the services available or products sold, the local council may need to be approached first and an approval obtained. Apart from certain exemptions (which may be found in relevant legislation or ordinances), a licence or permit is generally required for any advertising structure or sign. Many businesses overlook this area of control and spend money on signs which are then at risk if the council becomes aware of them. In the absence of an approval, the signs may have to be removed. Any refusal by council to grant an approval can be challenged in a court or planning appeal tribunal (provided the zoning of the council permits signs) but this can be time consuming and expensive.

Apart from its powers to prevent the business being conducted without a development consent or to remove a sign erected without approval, council may also instigate proceedings for breaches of certain town planning and local government law, which may result in a fine or penalty.

Be warned: local councils have wide ranging powers which can affect your business and it is dangerous to ignore these controls.

Pat Campbell is a partner in the Sydney law firm of Cutler, Hughes and Harris. You can contact him on (02) 9262 6799.

14. HIRING STAFF

"Only hire people you would be happy to have in your home and play poker with."
Dick Kress

Whenever he appointed a new head to one of his offices, David Ogilvy (advertising guru and head of the giant advertising firm Ogilvy and Mather) used to send them a set of Russian Matrioshka dolls. They are those brightly coloured wooden dolls that fit one inside the other, gradually getting smaller and smaller. Inside the smallest doll was a note which read: "If each of us hires people who are smaller than we are, we will become a company of dwarfs. But if each of us hires people who are bigger than we are, we will be a company of giants!"

Ogilvy simply wanted to demonstrate the point that you can achieve success by hiring people who are smarter than you are and managing and developing their skills. This is no easy task and very few people have the ability to do it well. Some people are afraid that if they employ somebody who is smarter or better than they are, it will be difficult to manage them. This is simply not the case. The world is full of ordinary people who have made a lot of money by simply employing people who are smarter than they are and managing their talent.

The greatest resource any business has is its people and employing the right people is critical to the success of your business. Employing the wrong people can be disastrous and costly. So, how do you go about hiring new people and what should you be on the lookout for?

Headhunting

One of the simplest ways to get new staff is to pinch them from somebody else! This might sound very unethical and of course it is. After all, the other company may have spent years and vast amounts of money training that person for the job. However, this practice has been going on for a long time and I have no doubt it will continue. At the big business level it is called *'headhunting'* and it is a sport that any company can play. It usually involves engaging a third party, such as a personnel consultant (or human resources expert if you prefer), and then getting him or her to approach a highly skilled person from an opposition company with a better offer. On a small business scale you would probably do the poaching yourself.

While the practice may be officially frowned upon in business circles, most large companies who have people poached from them have probably done a fair bit of poaching themselves, so it is generally accepted as 'normal practice' in the business jungle. The beauty of this method of recruitment is you get somebody who has the skills and experience and perhaps the contacts you need, without your having to go through the time and the expense of training them yourself. If you are going to go headhunting, however, be warned; there are a number of disadvantages to this method of recruitment, as follows:

Firstly, the person who allows themselves to be headhunted in this manner, is probably fairly mercenary and may well be head-hunted again by somebody else with a better offer than yours. Also, unless you have an intimate knowledge of the company and the person, they may well appear to be be more efficient and competent to an outsider than they really are. Another point - the person may be well trained in the methods of another business and could be reluctant to change their ways. This may not suit your organisation and you might be better off getting somebody who you can train to do it your way.

Friends and relatives

One of the most common mistakes small business people make when recruiting staff is employing friends or relatives who are not really suitable for the job. This can also make life very difficult later on, especially if you are required to sack the person, either through incompetence or because of a downturn in business. This can result in family rifts and people who used to be good friends becoming bitter enemies for life.

Many years ago I used to deal with a large wholesale firm in Sydney. Vic, the man who ran the business, was in my opinion an extremely good businessman and ran a very tight operation, with one major exception - the man driving his delivery truck. He was inefficient, lazy and totally incompetent. He just didn't seem to fit in with the rest of the organisation and eventually, curiosity got the better of me and I asked Vic how long this man had been working for him.

"Ever since I married his sister," he moaned! Be warned, friends and relatives don't mix too well with business.

One way of recruiting staff is to use an employment agency, and this will certainly save you a lot of time. As most agencies charge somewhere between 10 per cent and 15 per cent of the employee's first year's salary this can be a fairly expensive exercise but you need to weigh this against the cost in time of doing your own recruitment. If you do decide to place an ad in the paper and select the staff yourself, you can save a good deal of time by doing some preparation.

Here are a few tips:

• Prepare a written job description with details of all the tasks to be performed. List the attributes you are looking for on a piece of paper, number them in order of priority and then photocopy enough copies for each job interviewee.

• Give a score from one to ten for each of the major items and total them up. While you may not necessarily employ the one with the highest score, it will help you in your final evaluation. This is particularly useful if you are interviewing a lot of people, as it is sometimes difficult to recall the strong points of each individual.

• Have a sheet prepared for them to fill out when they arrive, listing where they worked previously and details of any referees. If they have already sent these details in before the interview, have these on hand and note any questions you need to ask.

• Look for gaps in employment. Beware of statements like: "two years working holiday travelling around Europe", etc. While they may well be quite genuine, if you have no way of checking it out, there's always the chance that they might be hiding something.

• Always thoroughly check any references, don't make the mistake of saying, "Well, they look honest enough".

• Have a list of questions prepared and try to make them open-ended rather than questions that can be answered with a simple *"yes"* or *"no"*. For instance, if the job requires meeting a lot of people and good people skills, instead of asking, "Do you like meeting people?" which would normally attract the obvious answer, you could ask, "What traits do you admire most in people?"

Instead of, "Do you think you would like the work here?" you could ask, "Tell me, why do you think you would like to work here?"

• Make sure you fully explain what the job entails and what is expected of the employee and give them every opportunity to ask questions. It is very important to make the interviewee feel comfortable and relaxed. Offer them a cup of tea or coffee early in the interview. Make sure you allow enough time between interviews and always be on time for appointments. Ask lots of questions and try to do more listening than talking.

• Always advise unsuccessful applicants as soon as possible after the interview. Thank them politely for making the application and wish them well in the future. Extend to them the same courtesy you would like extended to you if you were in their position.

Follow up
When you have completed your initial interviews and come up with a short list of the most suitable applicants, invite the chosen ones back for a further interview. It is surprising how much more you can learn about people in a second interview. For successful applicants, a letter of appointment should be written spelling out the terms and conditions of employment and again fully outlining the job description. This way there can be no problems later on with misunderstandings.

Finally, if you have good staff working for you, try to make sure you hang on to them. A large turnover in staff is very expensive, both in terms of time lost to find a replacement and in re-training. There is an old adage in personnel: *retaining* is better than *re-training*.

Staff involvement

One of the best ways to keep staff happy is to involve them in your business. Make them feel that they are a part of a team and their contribution is important and appreciated. Share your vision for the future with them. Many small business owners make the mistake of keeping everything close to their chest and not sharing their problems with the staff. Show that you are always open to new ideas and encourage staff to contribute their ideas, no matter how silly they might seem. A friend of mine offers a regular prize for the wackiest idea of the month, just to keep the staff thinking about new ways of doing things. Involve them in the decision-making process. Delegate responsibility and don't be too frightened to let go of the reins; remember, you can't do everything yourself.

Leadership

A good leader always leads by example. Don't be an 'armchair general', be prepared to roll up your sleeves, get in there and show them how to do it. Never ask the staff to do something you wouldn't do yourself.

In my early selling career, I worked for the Olympia Typewriter Company selling typewriters office to office. One of the most difficult parts of the job was getting past the receptionist to see the person in charge. As soon as you announced where you were from they would usually tell you they didn't want any typewriters and show you the door! The sales manager of the company at the time was a typical armchair general. When I told him about my problems, he said, "Just tell them you are from the OTC!"

The initials were right, the Olympia Typewriter Company, the OTC! Of course, people assumed I was from the Overseas Telecommunications Commission. It certainly got me past the receptionist and into the manager's office alright but can you imagine how they reacted when they found out where I was really from? They felt as if they had been conned, and rightly so! Not a very good way to start a relationship which you hope is going to lead to a sale!

After a day of getting thrown out of offices all over town, I went back to the sales manager and challenged him to come out with me for a day and show me how *he* could do it. He made some feeble excuse and declined. I promised myself from that day on that if ever I became a manager, I would never ask anybody to do something that I wouldn't do myself! I have tried to live by that doctrine ever since.

Summary

If you lead by example, good staff will follow you almost anywhere. This includes work habits. Don't expect to be able to go down to the pub for a three-hour lunch every day and have the staff do all the work. Even though you may be paying them well to do the job and you might feel this is your right as an employer, you will be disappointed if you take this approach. Staff like to see you doing as much work or more than they do. One of my favourite sayings in business is:

If you're a leader - lead, if you're a follower - follow and if you're not a leader or a follower - get the hell out of the way!

SECTION TWO:

MANAGEMENT

15. TIME MANAGEMENT

"The examples that have been held up to us in praise of work are a little unfortunate. 'How doth the little busy bee improve each shining hour, and gather honey every day from every opening flower'. Well, he does not! He spends most of his day in buzzing and aimless aerobatics and gets about a fifth of the honey he would collect if he organised himself."

Sir Henry Ogilvie

Learning how to manage your time effectively is one of the most important skills you can master in running a successful business. Most small business people spend far too much time doing things that don't have to be done or can be done by somebody else. You must learn to prioritise the tasks at hand and then allocate the available time accordingly.

There have been countless courses and books written about time management and many of them are excellent. The problem is you probably won't have time to do them or read them - you will be too busy trying to make a dollar!

Small business owners are often criticised for not taking time out to do courses and training and while this is a fair criticism in some cases, it often comes from people who have never run a business of their own and don't really understand the problem. Most small businesses, particularly in their formative years, survive on crisis management. No sooner do you put out one bushfire than another one springs up in another area. And it's the old story - *when you're up to your armpits in crocodiles, it's difficult to remember the purpose of the exercise was to bail out the swamp!*

So, how do you find enough time in the day to do all the things that need to be done?

Most of us overcome the problem by working longer hours and you will probably find this unavoidable. However, there are a few *'tricks of the trade'* that you can apply to help lighten the load.

Here's a million dollar idea:
One of the grandfathers of modern time management was an American with the memorable name of *Ivy Lee*. According to popular legend, Ivy Lee was engaged as a management consultant in the early 1900s by the head of Bethlehem Steel, Charles Schwab. Schwab told him that he wanted to become one of the biggest suppliers of steel in the US and asked Lee to work out a plan for him to achieve his goal. Eventually, he handed Schwab a sheet of paper. On it he wrote what was to become the simplest but most effective priority management system known to man. He simply advised him to write a list of the six most important things to do that day *(what we now refer to as a 'to do' list)*. At the end of the day, the list was to be reviewed and those items not carried out were to be transferred to the following day's list. Any item that stayed on the list for more than a week was to be deleted on the grounds that you were not serious about the task. Lee suggested that if Schwab could instill this simple concept into all his key managers, he would surely achieve his dream.

Schwab was initially a bit mystified and relatively unimpressed, "How much are you going to charge me for that", he asked?

Lee simply replied, "Try the system for three months and then send me a cheque for what you think it is worth".

Three months later, Schwab sent him a cheque for $25,000. *Taking into account inflation, by today's standards that would be equivalent to around one million dollars!* And Schwab went on to achieve his dream of becoming one of the biggest steel suppliers in America. There is no doubt that this simple task management system works. Try to implement it in your everyday life and you will be amazed at the results.

Another way of maximising your effectiveness, is to start a log book of how you spend your time, writing down each task performed during a given day and the time allocated to it. Review the results at the end of the day and decide which category each task falls into, then prioritise them as follows:

1. *Has to be done*
2. *Needs to be done at some stage*
3. *Nice to be done if there is enough time but not essential.*

Make sure that the bulk of your time is spent performing tasks in categories one and two. Be absolutely ruthless and cull all the time wasting jobs.

Here's another tip: when handling paperwork, operate strictly under the '4D' system, as follows:

DUMP IT
If it's not important, throw it in the rubbish tin and forget about it. Don't put it in your 'IN' tray and shuffle it around.

DELEGATE IT
If it is at all possible, get somebody else to do it.

DO IT
If it is a short job, can be done quickly, and has to be done, do it now and get it out of the way.

DECIDE WHEN TO DO IT
Set aside a time to do it and write it in your diary.

Work from a clean uncluttered desk. Don't have your desk piled high with papers and things to do. If you do chances are you will find yourself sorting through these things over and over again, which is in itself very time wasting. Jack Collis, a well known management trainer, gave me the following advice: "Every time you handle a piece of paper, draw a dot in the top right hand corner. When it gets the *measles*, burn it!" Great advice!

Use the 4D system and file anything that you are not working on. Put pens and pencils, phone books, diary, *'in'* and *'out'* trays, anything you don't need behind you, out of sight. Working from a cluttered desk can cause mental anguish and fatigue.

Don't go home with a desk full of papers. Clear the desk before you leave the office and write down your list of things to do for tomorrow. Transfer the items you didn't get done from today's list to tomorrow's list. Set aside a time each day for reading. Put reports or magazines or articles you want to read in your reading file, take it out at the allocated time and read it then.

Here's another simple tip: only keep one diary and write in it everything you have to do.

Get one that's small enough to carry around easily in your briefcase but large enough to record all your appointments and keep it handy at all times. I used to write appointments on my desk calendar and my wall calendar and I had a pocket diary and a great big diary on my desk in the office. The problem was, I often missed appointments because I forgot to transfer them from one diary to the other. If you have only one operative document, you won't have this problem. Now I carry one medium sized diary in which I record everything. I still have a wall calendar but I use it only for looking up dates and days and not for recording appointments. All my appointments (both business and personal) are recorded in this one diary.

Get a diary that opens on one full week at a time. This way you can see your whole week, Monday to Sunday, laid out in front of you. Plan your whole seven days, including your after hours and weekend leisure time. Sit down with your family regularly and set aside time for leisure and family events as well as your business appointments. Wherever possible, allocate a set time each day for the important jobs. Don't start the day by walking into your office or workplace and thinking - *what will I do first?* Plan your work and work your plan!

Summary
Make sure that every job you do maximises your best abilities and skills. If jobs like going to the post office, the bank or picking up the dry cleaning, etc., can possibly be done by somebody else, then make sure you delegate those jobs. Ensure that your time is spent doing the things that are going to provide the best possible dollar return to your business.

16. BAD AND DOUBTFUL DEBTS

"Credit is the only enduring testimonial to man's confidence in man."

James Blish

Should you decide to enter a business where you have to extend payment terms or credit, then you are more than likely to run into problems with bad or doubtful debts. And problems with bad debts are not just restricted to small business. Look at the massive amounts written off by the banks in recent years. It is very important to remember, a sale isn't a sale until you have been paid!

However, getting paid, and getting paid on time, isn't always easy. Unfortunately, these days it is often cheaper to write off a debt, even for several thousand dollars, than it is to pay the legal fees required to collect it! Worse still, it is possible to spend thousands of dollars on legal fees chasing a debt and then find it is uncollectable anyway and that you have simply poured more good money after bad.

There are a number of steps you can take to minimise bad debts. Good credit checking and chasing your debtors early, are two of the most important ones. Minimise your exposure by thoroughly checking out references and don't extend too much credit to one debtor, particularly if they look a bit shaky or are not well established.

Here's a useful tip: When you ask people to give you credit references, naturally they will only give you the names of people who are going to say good things about them. I have even known bad payer who have gone so far as to have a couple of '*special*' accounts that they always pay on time, just so that they can give out these names for credit

100

references. Try to find out the names of some of their other suppliers, especially the ones that they didn't offer as referees. Look at the brand name on their office equipment or if they are re-sellers of goods, note the names of some of their other suppliers. Try asking them where they buy their office supplies. If they start ducking and weaving there's usually a problem. Remember, even though you may be really keen to do business, there's not much point in making a sale if you are not positive of collecting the money.

Asking for money

Many small business owners are also their own sales manager or even the whole sales team, so they often have trouble in asking people for money. It's not easy to be calling on a client one day trying to sell them your goods and then ringing them the next day, asking for money. If this is your situation and you find it difficult to ask for the money, get somebody else to do it for you. You can hire somebody, perhaps on a part-time basis (maybe at the end of each month when you send out your statements) to get on the telephone and ask for payment. Get someone who is persistent, thick skinned and won't take *'no'* for an answer. When it comes to getting paid you sometimes have to be a bit ruthless. Know who the slow payers are and if you must extend them credit, at least limit the amount you extend to them.

If people don't pay or are slow - hassle them! After all, it could be a case of you or them! When it comes to getting paid, it is nearly always a case of the squeaky wheel getting the grease. I know of one small business owner who had a large amount of money outstanding and was having a lot of trouble collecting. He arranged for different staff members to ring the slow payers every morning and afternoon until they paid. It was a painful process but it got results in the end.

Trading terms

Important note: It is worth mentioning at this stage that the 'normal' trading terms in Australia tend to be 30 days from statement. This means that you issue an invoice when the goods are delivered and then you issue a statement at the end of the month. The client then has 30 days from the end of the month to pay you. Australia is one of the only countries in the world that operates on this system. Not only does it create extra paper work in having to send out statements, it gives the client an extra month or more to pay the bill. Try issuing a combined invoice/statement. Have a message printed on the bottom that says:

This is a combined invoice statement, no statement will be issued. Please pay 14 days from invoice date. Thank you.

It may not work with everybody but it is worth a try!

Settlement discounts

Some businesses have a policy of offering what is generally known as a *'settlement discount'* to people who pay on time or pay early. For example, this could be 2.5 per cent if the debtor pays in 14 days (instead of the normal 30 days).

My experience with settlement discounts has generally been fairly negative. I believe that the people who are most likely to take advantage of the discount are those businesses who would probably have paid you on time anyway. They are the big companies and institutions who have plenty of money. Chances are the slower payers won't pay any quicker because they can't afford to take advantage of the discount and some will even deduct it and still pay you late (or at least try to).

Another point to consider: it is pretty expensive money when you analyse it.

For instance, let's say that you offer 2.5 per cent for 14 days payment. If that client was going to pay you in 30 days anyway, that means you are offering almost a five per cent per month reduction. That's a whopping 60 per cent per annum! Even if they pay you 14 days instead of 45 days, that's still equivalent to nearly 30 per cent p.a. You would be better to invest this money in a better system of collection, e.g. employ a part-time or full-time collection person.

Collection agencies

When you start in business, from time to time you will probably be approached by various collection agencies, offering to collect your outstanding money for you. These agencies work on a percentage of the money they collect and therefore in theory, they don't cost you anything. *Remember, I did say in theory!*

You will find that some collection agencies work on the simple system that some money is easy to collect and some is hard to collect. You may find that you end up paying them a large percentage to collect the easy 50 per cent (who were going to pay you anyway) and you are still left with the hard to collect 50 per cent.

Collection agencies do offer a service and in some instances they can produce good results. And there are good collection agencies and mediocre ones. Some people are more likely to pay up on a demand from a collection agency than a demand from you. You can also get a solicitor to write a threatening letter, however it is far cheaper to collect the money yourself and better still, to avoid the money becoming too *'old'* in the first place.

When people are stalling payment, they will dream up every trick in the book. This ranges from the good old 'cheque's in the mail' to the more imaginative - *'the dog ate my cheque book'!*

You have to be a bit aggressive if you are going to collect your money. If someone says, "I'm putting a cheque in the mail to you right now", you should reply, *"Don't do that, we'll send someone around right now to pick it up and save you the cost of a stamp!"* Got the idea? Be a bit pushy!

Collecting your own debts
One of the alternatives to getting solicitors and collection agencies to chase your slow payers is to collect them yourself through the courts but be warned, it can be very time consuming. It involves going to the local court and applying for a summons. You will be asked to provide certain information pertaining to the debt, such as invoices, etc. You will be required to pay a fee (less than $100 at time of writing) for the preparation of the summons and the service of same by a sheriff's officer. The summons will then be served on the debtor and if they do not respond with a defence or pay their account within 28 days, you will be required to attend court and a judgment will be handed down, usually in your favour.

Once judgment has been awarded in your favour, the sheriff's officers can go into the premises of the debtor and seize goods or hold an instant auction on the spot and sell off their property (assuming they have any property). It is really quite severe.

A word of warning: I have been through this process a number of times and often it still gets back to the same old problem; if the debtor doesn't have any assets it won't help. This especially applies in the case of corporate debtors. You will often find that items of any real value (like a photocopier or computer for example) are on lease and as such are not owned by the debtor, they are still the property of the lessor.

A further word of warning: all of this takes time. Both time to go through the process and time to attend court. Once again you have to ask yourself the question: *is it worth it?* There may be times when you think that it is, just on principle. This might be so but don't lose sight of the fact that you can't eat principle! Once again, you can get a collection agency or solicitor to do all this for you but it can cost you a lot of money, whether you get a result or not.

'Professional' bad debtors

Unfortunately, there are people out there who realise the way the system works and they play the game to their full advantage. There are people who will tell you straight out, "Look, I haven't got the money and you can sue me all you like but you won't get a cracker!" The sad truth is, with these sorts of people it is often the case. They are what I call the *professional bad debtors*. They are sometimes protected by a company structure or they go into personal bankruptcy or simply disappear off the face of the earth without trace. Whatever the method, you end up whistling 'Dixie' for your money!

Sometimes the person owing you the money can be quite genuine. They really have gone broke, as a result of poor management or maybe even through no fault of their own. Perhaps one of *their* major creditors didn't pay *them* and they really don't have the money. Same result unfortunately - nothing but heartache for you.

Sometimes the company that owes you money is a large, long-established business. This type of bad debt is very difficult to avoid. You could try insuring your debtors through an indemnity policy but you may find the cost fairly steep and the insurer will usually require a fairly large minimum turnover before they are prepared to deal with you.

Summary

Without doubt, the best form of protection against bad debts is prevention. Get references from intending clients and check them out thoroughly. Join the *Credit Reference Association of Australia*. They have over two million records of Australian companies and their directors.

If you do have a client that suddenly starts to go slow on you, ring some of their other suppliers and see if they are experiencing similar problems. If the debtor owes money all over the place, get out early. Don't try to be a hero and help out by extending terms or further credit. Unfortunately, when it comes to debtors, my experience has been that *'nice guys'* usually finish last!

And finally remember, if somebody in business owes you money for goods or services you have provided, it's *your* money! You have every right to expect to get paid and to take whatever measures are necessary to recover any outstandings.

17. MATTERS LEGAL

*"A jury consists of twelve persons chosen to decide who
has the better lawyer."*
Robert Frost

Some years ago, I sold my retail electrical business to a good
friend of mine. It was his first venture into business and he and
his wife were extremely nervous about it and wanted to have every
possible situation covered. In the end, the sale became so bogged
down in legal red tape between his solicitor and mine, it was going
to cost more in legal fees than the business was worth. Eventually,
my solicitor (who was also a good friend and knew us both quite
well) said, "Hell, why don't you both just write each other a letter of
intent and leave the solicitors out of it?"

We did just that and fortunately for both of us, it all turned out
okay in the end. Not many solicitors would give you that sort of
advice. And I would certainly not recommend anyone else take this
course of action. If one of us had not played the game, we could
well have lived to regret it. More often than not, such a tale would
end in absolute disaster.

However, there are sometimes alternatives to using solicitors and
the courts, especially in cases of what are known as commercial disputes. Translated into layman's language, that simply means a dis-
agreement between two or more people in business. Sometimes disputes such as these can be resolved by both parties simply talking to
each other sensibly and trying to see the problem through the eyes
of the other person.

Alternative dispute resolution

If this fails, there are still alternatives other than to going through the courts, such as Alternative Dispute Resolution (ADR), which is a system that aims at bringing the parties in a dispute before an unbiased person, who acts as a mediator or an arbitrator. This person is usually not a solicitor (although he or she could be, more and more solicitors are getting involved in ADR). It should be remembered however, that just because somebody is a good solicitor this doesn't necessarily make them a good mediator.

ADR is usually a lot cheaper and quicker than going to court. It doesn't always work but the Australian Commercial Disputes Centre claims a very high clear-up rate at ten per cent of the cost and within five per cent of the time of litigation. It is also often possible to resolve a dispute and still maintain the goodwill of the parties, something that is almost impossible with litigation. It is a system that is gaining in popularity and little wonder when you look at the high cost of lawyers and the extraordinary length of time it takes to get a matter heard before the district courts (currently up to three years or even longer).

As a matter of interest, the Japanese are great believers in resolving disputes by mediation and they generally avoid going to court if it is at all possible. As a result, solicitors in this country (on a per capita basis) outnumber solicitors in Japan by sixteen to one!

You can access alternative dispute resolution by contacting the Australian Commercial Disputes Centre (ACDC), which has branches in most states or you can contact the following ADR associations:

Sydney: Australian Dispute Resolution Association
Melbourne: Mediation Association of Victoria
Queensland: Mediation Association of Queensland
South Australia: SA Dispute Resolution Association.

You may also find any of the following organisations helpful:

Conflict Resolution Network: Most major cities.
LEADR (Lawyers Engaged in Alternative Dispute Resolution)
Sydney, Melbourne and Brisbane.

If you would like to know more about ADR, you will find the following books useful:

Commercial Alternative Dispute Resolution
by Maxwell J. Fulton, and

Beyond Dispute
by Gordon Pears.

As a rule of thumb, avoid using the courts to settle disputes of any kind if it is at all possible. From my own bitter experience and that of many of my friends, usually the only people who win in a long and disputed legal battle are the solicitors. This is not to say that there aren't going to be times when you will need a good solicitor and sometimes you don't have a great deal of choice. And, let me stress that if you do find yourself in a situation where you have to engage a lawyer, then make sure you get a good one.

That doesn't mean you have to hire a Queen's Counsel to defend you on an illegal parking charge! Simply make sure that the counsel you hire is adequate for the job at hand. Under no circumstances should you ever defend yourself. The old adage that *'a man who defends himself has a fool for his counsel'* is generally very true. The system of law in this country seems to take into account the way in which cases are presented, as well as the question of guilt or innocence. Judges are usually very busy individuals and they can become very intolerant of people who are ill-prepared or want to play Perry Mason! This can weigh very heavily against you.

If you do become involved in litigation and you need to engage a lawyer, make sure you are dealing with someone who is experienced in the area of the law that you are involved with. These days the law is becoming more and more specialised. There are lawyers who specialise in litigation (lawsuits and disputations) and others who specialise in conveyancing (transferring property), industrial law or divorce. There are many areas of the law and it is definitely a case of horses for courses.

Note: The Law Society of Victoria recently moved to register certain solicitors as experts in small business and moves are afoot for other states to follow suit. Check with the Law Society or the controlling body of solicitors in your area. Bear in mind that these 'experts' are generally people who are skilled in the broad area of small business and it may still be necessary to retain an expert in a particular field, especially in cases where a large amount of money is concerned.

Summary
There will probably be a number of times during your business life when you will require the services of a lawyer. It is important to remember that in some ways, lawyers are a bit like dentists and doctors - the preventative method is usually the best. Just as the best time to visit the dentist is before all your teeth start to fall out, the best time to visit your lawyer is before you get into a mess. If you are going to sign an important agreement or document, get legal advice *before* you commit yourself. And just as you would with a doctor, if you are unhappy with the advice rendered, don't be afraid to seek a second opinion. While this may be expensive, it can pay off. A friend of mine approached a solicitor recently about a case of compensation and was told in no uncertain terms he had no chance of winning the case. Unhappy with this opinion, he sought alternative advice. The second solicitor had a completely different opinion and went on to fight the case and win compensation in the tens of thousands of dollars!

It must be stressed however, that this example is the exception rather than the rule and you should bear in mind at all times that good legal advice certainly doesn't come cheap.

18. INSURANCE

"The mechanics of running a business are really not very complicated when you get down to essentials. You have to make some stuff and sell it to somebody else for more than it cost you. That's about all there is to it, except for a few million details."
John L. McCaffrey

Making sure you have adequate insurance cover in case something goes wrong, is one of the most important aspects of running a business. Unfortunately, all too often small business owners don't consider all their insurance needs until it's too late.

There are a number of different types of insurance cover you will need to take out and while this will vary from business to business, depending on individual needs, some types are common to all businesses. The easiest way to ensure you are adequately covered for every possible problem is to appoint an insurance broker to take care of all your insurance needs. The only problem with this approach is, if the broker is tied to one major insurer you may find that you are not always getting the best possible deal on every type of cover. Some companies specialise in certain types of insurance and can therefore usually offer better rates or more comprehensive cover. This applies particularly to items such as motor cars.

To give you some idea of the variation between insurers, I recently wanted to take out insurance cover for fire and burglary on my office equipment (fax machine, computer, etc.). I rang one company and they said they would need to send down an assessor to inspect the building. They also wanted to know what type of alarm system we had (we didn't have one) and who had access to the building. To be insured with this company, I would have had to install an elaborate alarm system and better locks on the doors. In addition to all that they couldn't send the assessor for several days, which meant that in the interim period I wasn't covered.

I rang another very large company (one of the biggest) and they were quite happy to extend cover to me over the telephone! No inspection of the premises was required and no alarms or new locks and what is more, their rate was quite a good deal cheaper than the other company. As with most purchases, it pays to shop around. Of course, you should make sure that the company you are going to deal with is a reputable, well established firm. *It's not much use getting cheap insurance if they are not going to be around when you need to collect!*

While insurance requirements vary from one business to another, the following is a guide to the most common types:

• Material damage
Covers the assets of your business such as buildings, stock, plant and equipment against physical loss, destruction or damage. When arranging insurance, you should cover buildings and plant for their full replacement cost and allow for seasonal increases in stock values.

> *WARNING: When you insure your goods and stock for fire and burglary, make sure you insure for the full amount. Many insurance companies will only pay out on a pro rata basis. For instance, let's say if you had $1 million worth of stock and you insured it for only $500,000. If you had a fire and lost half of your stock, the insurance company may pay you for only half of that loss, i.e. $250,000, because you only had half of it insured! Make sure you read the fine print. Check carefully that you are fully insured in any event for the full amount of your loss.*

• Business interruption
Insures against loss of profit following material damage to the assets of your business. The increased cost of operating your business after such a mishap may also be covered.

• Burglary

Covers loss of or damage to stock, plant, equipment and other contents caused by burglars. Allow for seasonal increases in stock value. Check whether the policy also provides cover for damage to premises sustained in a burglary, costs of temporary security following a break in and replacement of locks should keys be stolen.

• Glass breakage

Breakage of fixed external and internal glass and other nominated breakable objects such as signs. Check whether the policy also covers damage to sign frames, replacing signwriting and ornamentation, damage to stock and costs of temporary shuttering.

• Money

Protection for money while in transit or on your business premises during and outside normal business hours, while in a locked safe and while in the private residences of authorised persons. Damage to safes and strong rooms may also be covered and seasonal increases in money held may also be allowed for.

• Public liability and product liability

Insures you against claims, for which you are legally liable, made on your business by members of the public as a result of death, injury or damage to property. You can also be protected against claims relating to the following:

- *the nature, condition or quality of products you sell or supply*
- *your liability as a tenant*
- *your liability for the goods of others left in your custody*
- *Employee dishonesty (enables you to insure against the risk of employees fraudulently taking money or goods belonging to your business).*

• Electrical mechanical breakdown

Allows you to insure nominated items of electrical and mechanical plant against sudden and unforeseen physical damage. In addition, refrigerated stock may be covered against deterioration following damage to insured refrigeration equipment.

• Computer and electronic equipment damage

Insures nominated computers and electronic equipment against sudden and unforeseen damage. Cover may also be arranged to meet data media restoration costs following loss of information from your computer's memory bank and the increased costs of maintaining a substitute data processing system after an insured equipment breakdown.

• General property

Covers specified property anywhere in Australia against accidental physical loss, destruction or damage. Valuable plant and equipment items taken away from your business location should be insured under this section.

• Motor vehicle

Covers specified motor vehicles against accidental damage and theft plus your legal liability for damage insured vehicles may cause to the property of others.

• Goods in transit

Gives you the choice of insuring nominated property while in transit in Australia against either loss, accidental damage or fire, flood, collision or overturning of the conveying vehicle.

• Personal accident and illness

Allows you to insure any number of specified persons. The cover may be for weekly benefits in the event of accident or illness or lump sum payments in the event of death or major disabling injuries caused by accident.

• Business insurance life plan

A life insurance plan can provide the cash required to repay a business loan on the death or disablement of a principal. Often such loans are secured by a charge over the business assets and the guarantees of the principals. Cash provided by the life insurance can discharge the business's liability, protecting the business assets and the estates of the guarantors.

113

• Key person insurance

Most business people are aware of the need to insure against loss of property or assets through fire or theft but they often overlook their most important asset - *people*. Key people are the most valuable asset of a business and you should consider insuring them. What would happen to your business if a key person became permanently disabled or died?

When taking out key person insurance policies, consideration should be given to any or all of the following scenarios:

- profitability decline due to the loss of key sales or production staff
- outlay of money needed to find a suitable replacement
- pressure placed on remaining staff and/or family members
- possible effect on credit if the bank becomes aware of the impact on the business
- the insecurity felt by remaining employees.

Life insurance arranged on the life of your key employees and owned by the business could provide a cash infusion in the event of the death or disablement of that employee.

Summary

The above list covers most of the common types of insurance risk but there may be additional risks depending upon your type of business enterprise. For instance, if you are importing or exporting goods, you could insure against foreign exchange losses (although often the cost of this type of cover is prohibitive) or if you are in the publishing business, you could insure against defamation. There are as many types of insurance cover as there are risks. Of course, the greater the risk, the more exposure the insurance company is subjected to and the higher the premiums will be. Similarly, the more you claim the more your premiums will rise. It is probably fair to say that most small businesses can't afford to insure for every possible risk situation under the sun but it can also be argued that they can't afford not to either. Many small businesses opt to leave some remote risks to chance but be warned: *a few dollars saved on insurance can be fatal for your business.*

A friend of mine has an electronic goods importing business and has never insured against burglary. He claimed his warehouse was an impenetrable fortress and he spent a small fortune on sophisticated alarm systems, etc. He often used to brag to me about how much money he saved each year on insurance.

Not long ago, a group of professional thieves struck at his warehouse one weekend. They actually removed a large section of bricks from the wall and with the use of a huge semitrailer, virtually cleaned out his entire stock. The result was devastating. A business that had taken him around twenty years to build up was virtually wiped out overnight. Even though the police later caught the thieves, very little of the stock was ever recovered.

Why take the chance? Better to spend the extra dollars on insurance and avoid the sleepless nights!

19. TAXATION

"Nothing in life is certain except death and taxes."
Benjamin Franklin

The above statement is certainly true for the life of your business, and nothing is more certain to get you into trouble than failing to meet your taxation obligations!

As well as income tax, if you are running your own business, you will almost certainly be subject to a number of other taxes. Check with the Australian Taxation Office (ATO) or your accountant as to which particular ones affect you. The following is a brief guide to the most common forms of business taxation:

Income tax

Any income you receive from your business will be subject to income tax. Your income is the amount that you earn in your business after deducting any legitimate and allowable expenses incurred in producing that income. What is and is not an allowable business expense is often the subject of contention. Typical deductible expenses are: *purchase of stock, wages, rent, advertising* and *freight*.

Non-deductible expenses include: *entertainment, personal purchases* and *personal expenses* (such things as holiday travel and even traffic fines).

One area in particular that can be a trap for new business starters is the purchase of capital equipment - such things as a computer or a motor car for instance. Generally speaking, such items are not fully deductible in the year of purchase. Goods such as these have to be

117

written down at a depreciated amount each year, over a certain period of time. Depreciation can be a complex issue and can vary depending on the item and its use. The amount you can claim can also vary from one year to the next. The ATO now publishes a list of the amount of depreciation it accepts as 'normal' on most business purchases. Many a small business owner gets caught in the capital equipment purchase trap.

For instance, consider the following scenario:

In your first year in business, you get to the end of the financial year and break even at the bank. i.e. you ended the year with the same amount of money in the bank as you started out with. However, during the course of the year you purchased a computer for $10,000, fully paid for with money out of the business. The maximum allowable deduction for this purchase in the first year is only 40 per cent* of the purchase price. Therefore, your claim on the computer is $4,000 and the balance of the purchase price ($6,000) would still be treated as income in that year, even though you have spent it on a legitimate business expense!

Depending upon your business structure, you could be asked to pay up to 48.7 per cent of this amount in tax, even though you no longer have the money. Of course, you can claim again for further amounts against this purchase in future years until you have written off the purchase but if you are operating on a tight cash flow this doesn't always help. Before purchasing any capital equipment, talk to your accountant about the various alternatives, such as leasing.

TIP: If you are going to buy a computer, don't just buy a complete package deal and then go along to a leasing company with your invoice. Software and maintenance are fully deductible in the year of purchase and therefore do not have to be amortised over a period of years.

Company tax
If you choose to operate under a company structure, any profits made in the company will be subject to company tax at 36 per cent*. Because the company tax rate is currently lower than the top marginal personal rate, there are still some major tax advantages in

operating a company structure. Once the company has paid tax on any profits, the balance can be paid to shareholders under the dividend imputation system as fully franked dividends and is virtually tax free or substantially tax free, in the hands of the receiver. Any losses incurred in the company can be carried forward into future years and claimed as a deduction on future profits.

Payroll tax

Payroll tax is one of the most hated and unfair of all taxes because it is effectively a tax on employing people. The more people you employ, the more tax you pay. Payroll tax is a state tax payable as a percentage of the money you pay out in wages. The amount payable varies from state to state and fortunately, it does not apply until your payroll exceeds $200,000 or more in most states, so many smaller businesses do not have to pay it.

Note: Check the threshold amount as it varies from time to time and from state to state.

Group tax

If you employ people, you will be required to deduct income tax instalments from their wages each week and remit this amount to the Australian Taxation Office within seven days from the end of each month. In order to become a group employer, you must first register with the Australian Taxation Office.

> *Be warned: Of all the taxes that you are asked to collect on behalf of the Government, group tax is probably treated by the ATO as the most important.*

Once you have deducted an amount from an employees wages for income tax, the Government considers that to be *their* money and they get very touchy if these payments are not made on time or records are not kept up to date and totally accurate. They have inspectors in the field who may call in and spot check you at any time. Substantial fines and even gaol terms apply for failure to comply.

Note: For smaller payrolls (at the moment, total annual group tax deductions of less than $10,000), you may submit these payments on a quarterly basis.

Prescribed payments system

This operates in a similar fashion to group tax but is available only for a limited number of industries, such as construction and cleaning. This system is usually used where the person carrying out the work is working as a contractor. In such cases, the ATO may require the person making the payments to deduct an amount for tax at a set rate. You must be registered to use this system. See your accountant or nearest branch of the taxation office for further details.

Fringe benefits tax (FBT)

Unlike income tax, FBT is payable by the employer not the employee - *mainly because if it were payable by the employee then the politicians and bureaucrats who made the law would have had to pay it themselves!* FBT is payable on any cash or non-cash benefit provided to any employee. It is payable at a rate of 48.4* per cent of the perceived benefit. Just to add to the confusion, FBT is payable under a different tax year to income tax and company tax (April to March) and is payable annually if your liability is less than $3,000 pa or quarterly if it exceeds this amount.

Typical items that would normally attract FBT are entertainment allowance, club membership fees, school fees paid for employees' children, subsidised rent, etc. Virtually any benefit that could be perceived as a form of payment in place of wages or a salary. Even discounts given to staff on purchases from their employer are considered to be a fringe benefit and may be subject to FBT.

Provisional tax

If you do not have a company structure and you are trading as a sole trader or partnership, you could be liable for provisional tax.

Provisional tax is a tax you pay on your projected income (over and above wages which you have already paid income tax on) for the next year. *In other words, tax on income that you have not yet earned!* This is calculated by taking your taxable income for the current year plus a projected increase on the same amount for the next year. Thus, you could find yourself liable for two years tax in your first year. This can be a disastrous or even fatal blow if you fail to make provisions for it. Talk to your accountant about the possible alternatives before deciding on your business structure.

Sales tax

Sales tax is payable at the last wholesale price on certain goods, either imported into Australia or manufactured here. If you are a wholesaler or manufacturer, you will be required to register with the taxation office and be issued with a sales tax number. If you are a manufacturer, you will be able to buy materials used in the manufacture of goods, tax exempt, by quoting this number or an exemption. You will then be obliged to charge sales tax on the last wholesale price and remit this tax to the federal government twenty-one days after the end of the month in which it was collected. Very small manufacturers or wholesalers with a notional annual sales tax bill of less than $10,000 may choose not to be registered and benefit from the small business exemption. Small manufacturers below a certain turnover can pay quarterly.

> *Warning: One of the big problems with sales tax is you are required to submit the tax on time, even if you have not been paid yourself for the goods. So if you are sending the sales tax money in and then getting paid 30 to 60 days later, it can put a severe strain on your cash flow.*

Capital Gains Tax (CGT)

If you build up your business and decide to sell it at some time in the future, any profits that you make over the original purchase price or establishing cost will be subject to what is known as capital gains tax. In fact, this is not a separate form of tax. It simply means that any profits on the sale will be treated as income and subject to income tax. New laws have been passed recently that now allow you to take part of the gain tax free, if you sell your business to retire or buy another similar business. CGT is a highly complex area and a lot will depend on the structuring of your business in the formative stages. Talk to your accountant and solicitor before you start or buy your business about the possible implications of CGT.

Rollovers

One of the big problems facing small businesses in the past has been the need to pay CGT on the rollover of a business.

For instance, if you sold one business to buy another business, the income on profit from the first sale was taxed at the full rate. Similarly, if a partner bought into your business, the amount he or she payed to become a partner would be treated as capital gain and taxed at the full rate. This discouraged people from selling their businesses and taking in partners and therefore stifled growth.

In the 1997 Budget, the Howard Government announced major changes to these laws. In certain circumstances businesses can now be exempt from CGT rollovers up to an amount of $500,000. This also applies where a person sells a business for the purposes of retirement. Consult your accountant or tax advisor for the latest ruling on these matters.

Important note: Any advice contained in this book is of a general nature only and should not be a substitute for professional advice. Check with your accountant, taxation advisor or the Australian Taxation Office (ATO) for the latest information. Rates of taxation and taxation laws are subject to constant change.

Note: the ATO puts out a number of very helpful publications for small business owners including 'A Tax Guide for New Small Businesses' and "A Guide to Keeping Your Business Records.' They are available on request at no charge.

20. RECORD KEEPING

"Money is something to make bookkeeping convenient."

H.L. Hunt, Texas oil billionaire

One of the areas where many small business owners get themselves into trouble is record keeping. Failure to keep precise and up-to-date records of all your financial transactions doesn't only mean you are likely to run foul of the tax man, it also prevents you from having an accurate picture of how your business is progressing. Constantly monitoring your business allows you to take action before it is too late.

A survey undertaken by the South Australian Government some time ago, discovered that as many as 30 per cent of all small business owners in that state kept no financial records at all in their first year of operation! This is a recipe for disaster. Good record keeping is essential to the ongoing good health of your business.

The Australian Taxation Office (ATO) requires you to keep receipts and records of expenditure for a minimum period of seven years. If you fail to do this and you are subject to a tax audit, you are not only liable to repay the amount of deduction you claimed, you will probably also be subject to a hefty fine. *Be warned: don't think it will never happen to you.* Think in terms of *when* I am audited not *if* I am audited. The ATO are recruiting more staff with the main purpose of auditing small business, so it is only a matter of time before they catch up with you.

Keeping records is even more important under the new regime of

123

self-assessment, where you are basically responsible for determining your own tax liability. Keep receipts and full documentation of every item of expense. Very small amounts of expenditure, such as parking meters or outside telephone calls for example, may be regarded as 'undocumentable' and a receipt is therefore not necessary *(diary notes could prove helpful)*. This is provided that:

- *the expense amount is less than $10*
- *the total of such expenses is less than $300 a year, and*
- *the Commissioner deems it unreasonable to obtain a receipt.*

For travel expenses, it is necessary to maintain a diary for each trip detailing the date of entry, the place visited and the nature of the activity, *e.g. attended conference*. These details should be entered into a diary as soon as possible after the activity occurs.

Keep it simple
It is essential that you establish a simple system of record keeping that is easy to maintain. If you do this early on in your business life and update it regularly, you will have much greater control over your business and your profitability. Don't make the mistake of leaving everything to your accountant; he or she can only do an effective job for you when you supply them with accurate information. It's not much good going to your accountant at the end of the year with a cardboard box full of receipts and records and expecting them to sort it out. Apart from the more obvious difficulties this creates in keeping accurate records of your business activities, it will also add significantly to your accountant's fees because of the amount of time needed to sort out the mess. As accountants charge by the hour, your job is to minimise their fee as much as possible by making their job easier.

Many small business operators find record keeping a painful and time consuming task but if you install a simple, workable system from the outset and keep it up to date, it will soon become routine. When you neglect it for a long time (and then have to sort through old records and receipts and try to remember what they were for), it becomes a long and tedious job that you tend to put off. This is how some businesses get hopelessly behind with their record keeping.

Your financial records are simply a way of recording two things:

- *where your income comes from, and*
- *what you spend it on.*

To start a simple record keeping system you will need the following:

- *a cash analysis book*
- *petty cash dockets (plus another cash analysis book to summarise the details)*
- *a concertina file (for receipts and dockets)*
- *a wages book*
- *invoices/statements*
- *receipt book*
- *cheque book*
- *bank deposit book*
- *a ring binder for your bank statements*
- *a diary.*

Write full details of any cash receipts or income received in your cash analysis book and on the butts of your deposit book.

On the outgoing side, make sure you get proper receipts for any expenditure. Wherever possible, pay by cheque, then record all expenditure details on the cheque butt and again in your cash analysis book. For regular items such as car expenses, it is a good idea to start an account at your local garage so that you have a statement every month of your purchases of petrol and any other vehicle expenses.

If you wish to claim motor vehicle expenses there are four different ways of claiming. See your accountant or the Australian Taxation Office for details. If you are going to be involved in sales tax or fringe benefits tax, you will also need to keep separate records for these items. In addition, if you employ staff or work for yourself under a company structure, you will be required to provide superannuation cover for those staff under the compulsory Superannuation Guarantee Charge.

Talk to your accountant before you start up in business and ask him or her to advise you on what records you need to keep and in what form they would prefer you to keep them.

I'VE WORKED IT OUT...
WE AREN'T OVERDRAWN,
JUST UNDERDEPOSITED...

21. COMPUTERS - ARE THEY REALLY NECESSARY?

"To err is human but to really stuff things up requires a computer."
Anon.

When I first wrote this book back in 1992, I questioned the need to buy a computer unless it was really necessary to either save time or produce income. I believe it was good advice at the time. However, since then, computers have become much more user friendly and the learning curve is not as steep. Also, the prices have tumbled dramatically and these days, it is difficult to imagine running a business without one. Even my local dry cleaning shop now records my details on a computer when I drop my clothes in. And, children in school these days are computer literate before they can read and write.

Computers can be of tremendous assistance to you in business but it is still important to decide which tasks you can do better on a computer that will save you time and money.

Here are a few ideas and recommendations on ways you can best use a computer in your business :

Controlling your finances
One of the best pieces of software I have ever bought is a simple program called *'Quicken.'* It allows you to take control of all your incoming and outgoing financial transactions. It is easy to use and allows you to print out reports and graphs on your income and expenses and it can even track accounts payable and pay roll.

At a cost of less than $100, this has got to be one of the most useful pieces of software you will ever buy.

Invoicing

If you are not going to generate a massive amount of invoices, there are a number of inexpensive *'off the shelf'* software packages that are relatively easy to use and will fulfil most of your invoicing needs. I use a program called *'Best Books'* which is again inexpensive and relatively easy to use.

TIP: *If you are not computer literate or you generate a lot of invoices, you might be better off using a bookkeeping bureau to do this for you. There are plenty of them around and their costs are usually very reasonable. This will free your time up to do more productive things like concentrating more on the sales and marketing.*

Word Processing and other uses

A combination package like *Microsoft Works* or *Claris Works* is a good investment. Both of these packages include a basic word processor (for writing letters, etc.) and a spread sheet program, for doing things like cash flow projections and budgets. Both of them also include a database management program however, you may find it better and easier to buy a separate program for this use.

Database Management

One of the most valuable (but often overlooked) uses for computers in small business, is building a database for promotional purposes. It usually costs five times more to get a new client than it does to retain an existing one so, it makes sense to maintain regular contact with your existing clients.

Put your clients into a database on your computer and mail them regularly. Send out a regular newsletter and list details of your special offers and any new products or services. Explore the possibility of buying a mailing list from a list broker *(you will find these listed in the Yellow Pages)* and mail out promotional material or you could just list names from the telephone directory and record the results of each call. Record your customer's birthdays and special events and send them cards. You can even send them a regular note simply saying: *"Thanks for continuing to do business with us!"* These personal touches help you to build long-term relationships with your customers and done properly, they can instill tremendous loyalty and lead to referral business.

Several extremely good off the shelf database management programs are available for around the two or three hundred dollar mark. *Tracker* is an good contact management program or check out *FileMaker Pro* or *ACT* if you want to take it a step further.

Desk Top Publishing

Here particularly, I would like to sound a note of caution. Since the advent of desktop publishing on computers, some people think they can become overnight graphic artists. And, some of the worst examples of their work look positively awful. Even though you may be technically proficient, design, typography and page layout are skills that are best left to the experts. There are any amount of small (often home-based) graphic artists, that will produce a professional looking result for a very modest charge. I believe this is a good investment and usually a better alternative. Unless you are particularly good at it, invest in some expert advice, it is usually well worth the cost. *And remember, you only ever get one chance at a first impression!*

Summary

If you do decide to buy a computer, don't just rush out and buy the first package deal you see offering lots of free software. Decide first what you are going to use the computer for and then choose the best software for the job. Then, buy a computer that is suitable to run that software. Shop around, talk to other people in your industry and ask them what type of computer and software they use and if they are happy with it.

TIP: Computer software is fully tax deductible in the tax year that you buy it, while hardware (the machinery itself) is not. Therefore, if you buy a package deal of software and hardware, get the company you buy it from to break down the cost of each item on your invoice so you can claim the full amount of the software. *(see the chapter on Taxation for further details).*

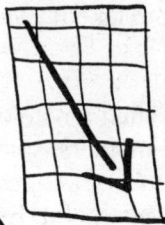

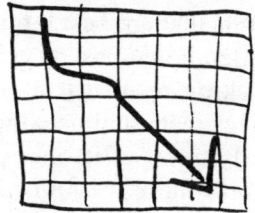

SECTION THREE:

SALES, ADVERTISING AND PROMOTION

22. THE SALES CHALLENGE

"Nothing happens until somebody sells something."
Anon.

One of the most daunting tasks for many people starting their own business, is facing the prospect of having to get out there and sell their wares. However, with a little understanding of the principles involved and some basic training, anyone can become a successful salesperson and *(believe it or not)* even learn to enjoy it!

Sales are the lifeblood of your business. Many small firms go to the wall simply because they don't sell enough of their goods and services. Whether you are taking over an existing business or starting a new one from scratch, the success of your venture will most probably rely heavily on your ability to make sales. Unfortunately, most people – particularly those who don't have previous experience in sales – find the thought of having to *sell* something to somebody quite daunting. This phobia is usually attributed to the fear of rejection but it is really caused more by a lack of understanding of the sales process.

What does it take to become a successful salesperson?
People generally have preconceived notions about 'typical' salespeople. They see them as young, slick, fast-talking people, someone who could sell ice blocks to the Eskimos! While there are plenty of salespeople around who fit this image quite well, they are not typical, nor are they necessarily successful. Most of the successful salespeople I know all look and talk like ordinary people.

That's because they are ordinary people and this actually contributes to their success.

People will only buy from you when they trust you and they are more likely to trust you if they feel that you are just like them. Don't try and assume a personality that's not you. Chances are you will feel uncomfortable and your discomfort will show through as insincerity. You are far more likely to be successful at selling if you remember the golden rule: *be yourself.* To get people to trust you, you need to be sincere, and the best way to achieve this is to tell the truth and be yourself.

The most commonly held misconception about selling is that salespeople sell things to people whether they want to buy them or not. This is just not true. In fact, nobody ever *sells* anything - people *buy!* Customers only need to be convinced of the benefits of ownership. Once customers are convinced that the benefits of buying are worth more than their hard-earned cash, they will buy from you, not a moment before.

Your job as a salesperson is to assist them in their buying decision by presenting sufficient evidence to support your case. You simply have to demonstrate the benefits of ownership. This is called *selling the sizzle, not the sausage.* For instance, people don't buy a new car - they buy a better form of transportation. They don't buy an electric razor - they buy a closer shave and a better appearance. Take a look at television ads. They don't sell beer - they sell having a great time with your mates. In other words, they sell the benefits of ownership, not the product itself. So as a salesperson you are, in effect, the *'assistant buyer'.* You help people to get what they want and through this process, you get what you want, therefore it's a win/win situation.

What motivates people to buy?
People buy when they are going to gain something. This could be profit or personal gain. It could be prestige or status or sheer pleasure. If they are buying for someone else, then it is simply one or more of those benefits applied to the person they are buying for.

There is also another reason people buy - *fear.*

This could be fear of what could happen if they didn't buy the product, for instance, life insurance or health care services. It could be fear of missing out on a possible bargain or advantageous position. All buying decisions are generally made for one or more of the above reasons.

THE FIVE STEPS
Let's analyse the five basic steps that make a sale:

Step 1. Define your prospect
These are the people who have a need for your product or service. Remember, selling is a numbers game. The more people you talk to, the more sales you will make. Assuming, of course, that you have a saleable product and reasonable presentation skills, and that the person you are talking to has a genuine need for your product.

Step 2. Qualify the prospect
Make sure you are talking to the decision-maker. So many salespeople waste their time talking to the wrong person. Make sure you are talking to the right M.A.N. – that's an acronym for the Money to buy, Authority to purchase and Need for your product.

Step 3. Do the presentation
Know your product inside out, not only its good points but its limitations too. This will enable you to anticipate objections and overcome them, which leads us to the next step.

Step 4. Overcome objections
Convince them of the benefits. Remember, objections are really buying signals. For instance, if a customer says, "It's too expensive", what he or she might be really saying is, "I like the product but I am not yet convinced that I should pay that much money for it. Tell me more..."

Step 5. Close the sale
Any sales manager will tell you that many sales are lost simply because the salesperson failed to *ask for the order*. Most sales trainers advise closing early, closing late and closing often! Zig Ziglar,

the famous American motivational speaker and sales trainer, claims that most sales are made the *fifth* time you ask for the order. This is not as daunting as it may sound. You can try asking for the order with a *'trial close'* at any time during your sales presentation. For instance: "Would you like it in red or green?" If they indicate a colour preference – *"Does it come in blue?"* they are virtually saying, "Let's do business!"

Here is an important point. If they are not convinced, you must introduce more benefits before you try to close again. It is no use simply asking for the order over and over again like a mindless robot. You must present new evidence and give more reasons to buy on every rejection before trying to close the sale again. This brings up another important point: *successful sales people do a lot more listening than talking.* Remember, the Lord gave us two ears and one mouth so that we could *listen* twice as much as we *talk!* There's an old adage in selling that says, nobody ever *listened* themselves out of a sale!

Summary

Listen to what your prospect is saying and look for buying signals and hidden objections. Most people love to hear the sound of their own voice. By allowing your prospects to talk, you not only learn more about their needs and wants, you give yourself time to think and consider your next course of action. Encourage the prospect to talk by nodding every now and then and saying words like, "yes" or "right". As with any other skill, practice makes perfect, so don't get discouraged if you don't make sales on your first few calls. Don't get bitter, get better! And remember, every time somebody says *"no"* you are one step closer to getting a *"yes"*.

Listen to tapes and read books on selling. Get a copy of Tom Hopkins book, *"How to Master the Art of Selling,"* it is one of the best books on selling ever written. If your business relies heavily on making lots of sales, get some professional sales training. Join your local SWAP Club - Salespeople With A Purpose, if you have one in your area (check your local telephone book) and attend seminars and workshops on selling.

And, don't forget - *nothing happens until somebody sells something!*

23. ADVERTISING

*"Doing business without advertising is like winking at
a girl in the dark - you know what you're doing but
nobody else does!"*
Stewart H. Britt

How to advertise and promote your wares is probably one of the
most complex problems you will ever have to face in running
your own business.

American retailing guru, John Wanamaker, probably summed up
the frustration of business people the world over when he made the
statement, *"Half of all the money I spend on advertising is wasted –
the only trouble is I don't know which half!"* And if he didn't know,
what hope does the average small business owner have? What's
more, small business operators are at a considerable disadvantage
over their big business counterparts, who usually enlist the help of
professional advisers in the form of an advertising agency.

Unfortunately, most advertising agencies don't want to know you
unless you're spending hundreds of thousands of dollars a year on
advertising. Even a business spending $100,000 a year would
probably still be considered more of a nuisance than a benefit to a
large agency. You may be able to find a small agency that is
prepared to take you on and grow with you but the main problem
with small agencies is they are generally limited in their areas of
skills. A good alternative could be to find somebody in the industry
who wants to do a little bit of *'moonlighting'*.

Ian Oshlack, in his book, *'Advertising Without Agencies'*,
suggests a good way to find moonlighters is to pick up a copy of *Ad
News* or *B & T* magazine. In it you will find articles about great

advertisements. They always list the names of the people who worked on the ads and their agencies. He suggests you could approach them direct and see if they are interested in doing a bit of work for you after hours. It's a bit cheeky but he claims you might be surprised at the response.

Prime Prospect Profiles

Because of the high cost and the degree of difficulty in getting good, unbiased advice, many small business people choose to do their own advertising or at least choose the method of advertising themselves and then get help with things like art work and production.

Your major advertising problems will probably centre on two major questions:

- *how much should you spend*
- *where should you spend it?*

Before you find the answers to these questions, you must first determine who your target audience is. This is what is termed as your *Prime Prospect Profile* or PPP. In other words, the people most likely to have a need for your product or service. Most importantly, who are the people who actually buy the product? *Note: this may not necessarily be the same people who use it – for instance, men's underwear is predominantly bought by women.*

In order to define your PPP, you will need to ascertain the following information about your potential customers:

- *age range*
- *sex*
- *geographical location (where they live or work)*
- *ethnic background (if applicable)*
- *any other information that makes them unique.*

The Australian Bureau of Statistics (ABS) offers a tremendous service called *'4-site'* that can help you with this exercise. For a modest fee, using their massive bank of data they will provide you with colour coded maps showing the exact location of almost any type or group of people. This can include such information as ethnic origin,

137

number of children, average income per home, etc. Almost anything you need to know about the population of Australia. This vast source of information can be of tremendous assistance to your business.

For instance, let's say that you wanted to start an accountancy practice and you spoke fluent Italian and Spanish. The ABS could tell you which suburbs have the highest proportion of people who speak Italian or Spanish in the home and you could then locate your business accordingly.

Once you have established your target audience, you can then start to think about which type of media will be the most cost effective in reaching them, and how much you will have to spend to achieve the desired result.

How much should you spend?
How much you need to allocate to advertising will vary dramatically from industry to industry. Most industries have an accepted *'industry norm'* for the ratio of advertising spent in relation to turnover and this is usually measured as a percentage of gross sales - check with your industry association for details. If you don't have an industry association, ask other people in the business what percentage they spend or ask your local Chamber of Commerce or Small Business Agency for advice. Your accountant should also be able to give you a good idea of what is reasonable.

The amount of money spent on advertising can vary, from as low as one or two per cent in some businesses to as high as 10 per cent or even more in certain cases. For most industries however, somewhere between two and five per cent of gross sales would not be considered excessive, particularly for a new business trying to establish itself.

How much you spend should be directly tied to your sales results, however it should be stressed that in advertising it is very easy to spend money in the wrong way and virtually waste the lot. It's not simply a case of saying, *'you get back what you put in'*. Eventually you will discover how much you need to spend and where to get the best result but trial and error is an expensive way to learn. In the first instance it is usually safer to go with the more conventional approaches and see what sort of results you get before attempting anything too adventurous.

Allow time for an advertisement to work. This doesn't mean you should stick with an ad indefinitely if it is not producing a result but you can't always expect a huge immediate response. If you are getting a fair response and it is improving every time you repeat the ad, then stay with it. Often it takes a long time for people to get the message so, if you've got an advertising campaign that's working, don't change it just because you or your staff are sick of it – make sure the customers are sick of it first. *And remember, when they are sick of it, chances are it will work even better!*

Layout and design

If you are doing your own advertising in the press, try to come up with a good headline that will attract people's attention. Research has shown that people only ever read around eight per cent of a newspaper (the parts that are of direct interest to them). They select what they are going to read by scanning the headlines of both the ads and the editorial. It has been estimated that 80 per cent of people will read no further than your headline. Try to come up with something interesting and different but don't get too clever. Look for your unique selling proposition (USP). What is it about your product or service that makes it a better proposition than your competitor's? Is it price, convenience, service, quality, time saving?

If you don't have a USP then set about creating one! You have to come up with a reason why people should buy from you rather than your competitors. In other words, what are the major benefits? List your major benefits and then try to incorporate these into your headline. Keep your message short and simple. There is a formula for a good advertisement which works on the initials of the opera AIDA. They stand for:

ATTENTION
INTEREST
DESIRE
ACTION

You should apply the AIDA test to all your advertisements before you place them.

For instance, in a press ad you would use the headline to grab their attention. Then the subheading or the graphic (photo or drawing) might be used to create their interest and the body copy of the ad should create the desire for ownership. And finally it should call them to action. Introduce a note of urgency: *Buy before the end of this week and save 20 per cent* or *limit of 100 units only until sold out.* And don't forget to tell them where they can get it. A statement such as, *pick up that phone and call us right now on 123456* or *call in to our showroom at 14 High Street today.* And don't be afraid of using too many words. If the copy is interesting and your proposition is good, people will read it.

Circulation and distribution
Advertising is never a cheap exercise, so try to make sure you get your money's worth. Newspaper advertising rates are usually measured on a cost per thousand basis (CPM). This means the amount it costs to reach each one thousand people. To arrive at this figure, simply divide the circulation of the newspaper into the cost of the ad and multiply it by 1,000. For instance, let's say you placed a $500 ad in your local paper and it had a circulation of 40,000. Divide 500 by 40,000 and you get 0.0125, then multiply this figure by 1,000 and you get the answer 12.5. This means the cost of advertising in that paper is 12.5 dollars ($12.50) per thousand readers.

Bear in mind, you must establish the quality of the readers as well as the quantity. There's not much use having thousands of readers if they don't have a need for your product or service. And don't forget circulation doesn't necessarily mean readership. Just because somebody tosses a paper over your fence every week doesn't mean to say you are going to read it, especially if it is a rainy day and it got wet or the dog chewed it up!

Similarly, be very wary of trade magazines and newsletters that deliver free copies to members of associations and organisations. I don't know about you but I get a number of publications delivered to me in the mail that I don't even bother to take out of the plastic wrapper! If people have to *pay* for a publication they are far more likely to read it.

Of course, the best measure of an advertisement's effectiveness is your bottom line. Monitor your results carefully and when you find something that works, keep doing it until it stops working. To use the words of an old fly spray commercial - *when you're on a good thing, stick to it!*

Advertising and location

The best time to consider how much you will have to spend on advertising is before you decide on the location of your business. The amount of money you pay in rent per square metre is usually directly proportional to the amount of money you will have to spend on advertising, particularly if you are entering into a retail business. There is an old adage in retailing that says the three most important ingredients for success are: *position, position and position!*

If you are going to be in a retail business and you are located in a poor position for passing trade (a situation I would strongly advise against), you may need to spend a veritable fortune on advertising just to get people through your front door.

So in calculating the amount you will need to spend on advertising, you must take into account your location and the degree of difficulty you will experience in telling potential customers where you are and what you are doing. Some retail shops in the heart of large shopping centres, for instance, may undertake not to spend any money on advertising at all, relying simply on the high volume of passing trade created by the shopping centre. In other words, their rent to some extent becomes their advertising budget! However, these people are often required to pay into a merchants' fund (this is where all the shopkeepers in a centre pay into a slush fund which is used to jointly promote the centre).

From my own experience it is usually better to pay a higher rental and be in a good position where you can rely on a large passing trade, than it is to go for a cheaper location and rely on spending big money on advertising to draw people in. This is simply because in the first instance we have a known factor - the number of people who will pass by (and hopefully enter) your front door. In the second instance, we are relying on our ability to produce advertising that gets results. The big disadvantage with the high rent scenario is that you can't reduce the rent but you can cut back on the advertising budget.

If you have a product that appeals to a broad spread of the population, then your best choice will probably be to go to a very busy

141

location and simply play the numbers game i.e. *the more people that go past the door, the more people that buy.* Of course, this doesn't always work in practice, but at least you are loading the odds in your favour and you won't need to spend a lot of time and effort on advertising campaigns.

One important word of caution here: passing trade does not necessarily include motorists driving past your door, especially if there is difficulty in stopping or parking. Plenty of retailers have gone broke on major highways with thousands of cars passing them by every day. It's not much use unless they can pull over and park with relative ease and safety.

My first venture into my own business was a TV and radio shop in the city of Sydney. I had the choice of either renting a shop in the central business district for around $2,000 a week or setting up on the city fringe for around $500 a week. I chose to go for the lower rental and spend the extra money on advertising. While the shop did reasonably well, I later realised that had I opted for the CBD I would have sold three or four times as much product without any advertising at all. I also hadn't taken into account the cost of advertising in the city. Because my target market was primarily city office workers, there was no 'local' paper as such and I was forced to use the metropolitan daily newspapers and radio stations to reach my audience (which was mainly city workers). This meant very high advertising costs and a great deal of wastage because a big percentage of the audience were too far away from my business to bother responding to my ads.

Advertising is not a science and it can be a very 'hit and miss' affair. There are countless cases in the advertising history books of companies that have spent millions of dollars on advertising and still failed to create the desired result, even with the assistance of the so-called experts. It is not uncommon to place an ad in a newspaper at high cost and receive little or no response.

Niche markets

If you have a product which is very specialised and has limited appeal to a small number of people, you will probably be better off going to a cheap location and relying on local advertising and word of mouth to build up your trade. For instance, a shop specialising in school uniforms for specific schools, could choose a location strategically close to the schools concerned rather than a high rent area. This would depend on forming a close association with the schools; ideally they would recommend purchasing from you and perhaps allow you to distribute leaflets to the parents or advertise in the school magazine, etc. In such a case, you would be able to reach your potential audience cheaply and effectively. The cheaper rent could allow you to sell your goods at a lower price than your competitors and if you passed this saving on to your customers, this may allow you to build a strong business in a small but captive market. This is what is known as *'niche'* marketing, where you are catering to a smaller, specialised segment of a market, rather than the whole broad market.

Choice of media
If your business is going to appeal to a broad audience, then your selection of media becomes much more difficult. There seems to be a thousand and one ways to advertise. For instance, there's TV, print, radio, outdoor signs, direct mail, pamphlets, cinemas, public relations, bonus coupons, directories, premiums, exhibitions and transport ads. You can even have your message written in the sky by a plane or displayed on the back of a toilet door! (*A thousand and two?*)

When starting out, it usually pays not to be too adventurous in your choice of media. This doesn't mean that you can't be creative. It means that unusual or unproven media are probably too risky and should generally be avoided. The most obvious choices will be the Yellow Pages telephone directories, pamphlet drops or the local paper. If you can identify your market clearly and have access to a good list of prospects, direct mail can be highly effective, especially if it is followed up with a telephone call.

Generally speaking, radio and the metropolitan daily newspapers produce far too much wastage for the average small suburban business. Unless your offer is totally unique or very price competitive, most people won't travel more than a few miles from their local area for their general needs.

One very effective form of promoting business that is often overlooked is face to face calling. Often small business owners spend a fortune on advertising their services to the world but wouldn't even

143

think of asking the surrounding business houses if they could be of assistance. This simple act sometimes produces amazingly good results. This is partly because convenience is one of the most important factors in the purchasing decision. You will also find that other business people will have a certain degree of empathy with you when you are new in business (they were new themselves once), and they will often tend to *'give you a go'*.

In many cases, the simplest ideas work the best. This may be as basic as painting a big sign on the window of your shop or handing out leaflets with a special offer. Good signage and identification can play a major role in boosting business and need not cost a fortune.

I recently went to drop in some artwork to a friend of mine who runs a small printing business. Although he has a shop front on a very busy main road, I had a great deal of trouble finding him. This was because one side of his front awning was painted out with a sign for a newsagency and the other side had a sign for a video shop, both obviously from previous tenants. The only sign for his business was a small poster in the window, about half a square meter in size, which was difficult to see from the street. I pointed out to him that it wouldn't cost much at all to repaint the awning in a bright colour and if he stuck a sandwich board or one of those signs that spin in the wind out the front saying "PRINTER' he would probably be surprised at the results. Better still, what about a sandwich board out front or a big sign on the window with a red hot special offer on business cards? Every business needs calling cards and once they came to him for the cards, they would need other items of printing too! All simple common sense stuff and it works.

Summary

The main thing with advertising and promotion is to keep at it, try new approaches or a different slant to an old idea.

Remember, business is like a wheelbarrow– it stands still unless you keep pushing it!

Every dollar you spend on advertising in a small business should be designed to give you the maximum return in sales for your investment. Your sole purpose for advertising should be to bring in more business as quickly as possible. This means that corporate or institutional advertising (just keeping your name in front of the public or telling them what nice people you are) is generally a no-no. Leave that to the BHPs and Shell Oils of the world – it's a luxury you can't afford.

Your advertising message should contain some sort of an offer or a unique selling proposition. It should state why you do it better, cheaper or quicker than the others. Statements like *'free'* - *'special offer'* - *'fifty per cent off'*, etc., while seemingly done to death, still produce results if they are genuine offers. People love to think they are getting a bargain, especially in tough times. Something like forty per cent of all the merchandise sold in large department stores these days is generated from their sale catalogues. Why do you think they keep doing them? *Because they work!* Make your advertising dynamic and hard-hitting and aim to get a measurable result from every cent you spend.

And one final word of warning: make sure that the product or service that you advertise lives up to your claims. How many times have you responded to an advertisement yourself, only to find that the advertiser (or the staff of the advertiser) didn't seem to care whether you bought the product or not? Make sure that your telephone is answered in a professional and courteous manner and that enquiries are followed up promptly. Remember – there's not much point spending money on advertising if you aren't going to capitalise on the response.

24. THE NAME GAME

*"What's in a name? That which we call a rose by any
other name would still smell as sweet."*
William Shakespeare

The above quotation from Shakespeare may be true of roses but
when it comes to starting and building a business, the choice of
an appropriate name can be more critical than you might think.

In choosing a name, a number of considerations must be made.
Firstly, the name should be easy to remember, easy to find in the
telephone book (try finding 3M or 2UE) and ideally, it should be
synonymous with what you do. Having said that, a number of people
may wish to challenge this observation with various examples of
companies with names that do not fill any of the above criteria and
yet have still been enormously successful. For example, what about
the photocopying people Xerox? The name Xerox, is a difficult
name to remember, extremely difficult to find in the telephone book
(unless you know how to spell it) and it has virtually nothing directly
to do with photocopiers in the generic sense, as far as I know.
(Although the name did eventually become a generic name for
photocopying, as in, *"Xerox this"* meaning to photocopy something).

*Why then has Xerox been so successful in selling their name,
image and product to the public?*

The answer is simple and can be largely explained by one word,
money! A well known advertising guru once said if he had a big
enough advertising budget he could sell tuberculosis! If you have
enough money and you persist long enough, you can probably be
successful with virtually any choice of name at all, providing of
course the product or service is up to scratch. Xerox was one of the

146

first companies in the world to use prime time television for a commercial product (rather than a domestic consumer product). Up until that point, most companies in this field had generally only ever advertised in daily newspapers and trade magazines.

Would Xerox have been more successful in the photocopying business if they had adopted a name that was synonymous with the business they are in? For example, what would have happened if they had adopted a name like *Copymaker* or some other name that told people what they did? The answer to that question will never be known but one thing we do know is this: *a name alone doesn't automatically sell a product, no matter how well known it might be.*

When Xerox decided they wanted to expand their business by entering the fiercely competitive computer market, they virtually fell flat on their face. It has been estimated that Xerox spent over one billion dollars trying to break into the computer market before finally retiring to lick their wounds and rethink. Xerox apparently did such a good job of selling themselves in the photocopying market, people were just not prepared to accept them as a viable manufacturer of any other product.

The importance of names

If you are just starting out in business, chances are you won't have millions of dollars to spend promoting your name, so your choice of an effective name becomes even more important.

A clever and imaginative name can get people talking about you and generate a lot of word of mouth advertising for your business. A good example of a clever name like this is a Manchester shop in the Sydney suburb of Newtown called *Holy Sheet.* I have lost count of the number of people I have personally told about this place. I don't know if any of them have actually ever been inside and bought anything but at least their name has got people talking about them. I certainly wouldn't have mentioned it if their name had been *Maud's Manchester Shop* or something equally as boring.

It is usually a good idea to make sure that the name you have chosen conveys an image of what you do. If you can also include some additional information that briefly tells people why they should buy from you and why your business is a better alternative, then so much the better.

For instance, if you are going to enter a market with a lot of price competition, you can convey the image that you are cheaper than your competitors by including that message in your name. *Budget Carpet Cleaning* or *Cut Price Carpet Cleaning,* sound as though they might be cheaper than *F & J Applegate's Carpet Cleaning Service.* The words *Budget* or *Cut Price* certainly give the impression that you are prepared to talk about price and are not at the top end of the market. Other words like *Cheaper* or *Cheapa* or *Discount* can be used to create the same effect.

Of course, these words can also convey poor quality or rough-and-ready workmanship. If you are aiming more at the high quality end of the market you could try incorporating words that portray an image of high quality and service. You could be *'Distinctive'* Carpet Cleaning or *'Quality'* Carpet Cleaning. On the other hand, you may decide to tell people that you are a *'Reliable'* Carpet Cleaning Company or a *'Dependable'* one.

Maybe you would rather promote the idea that you offer quick service. In this case you could be *'Speedy'* Carpet Cleaning or *'Quick'* Carpet Cleaning or maybe even *'Kwik Karpet Kleaning'.* A word of caution here: if you are going to use modified spelling, such as *Kwik* instead of *Quick,* this will make you hard to find in the telephone book. If somebody recommended your name, "Call the Kwik Karpet Kleaning Kompany, they're good" - it won't help you if they forget to tell people that it is spelt with a *'K'* rather than a *'Q'* because they will never be able to find your name in the telephone book!

The examples given above are very obvious ones and are designed to get you thinking. In choosing your actual name you may decide to be a lot more subtle in implying the type of quality and service you are going to provide. For instance, *International* sounds like you are big or words like *Professional* or *Supreme* conjure up images of better service.

By the way, if you do choose a name of this nature, it is important to make sure that you can live up to your claims. There's not much point in being the *'Quicker Plumbing Service'* if you are going to arrive two days after the call to find the house under water!

My good friend and marketing guru Ken Smithson, tells a great story about business names that I particularly like; it's about *Harry Tubshaw's Furniture Removal Company*. Harry was in the domestic furniture removal business and was going broke fast. Most of Harry's work was done on weekends and a large percentage of his workforce was made up of casual students from the local university, trying to earn an extra dollar. One day, Harry hit on a bright idea. He changed the name of his business to *The Hungry Students' Furniture Removal Company* and never looked back! The public just loved the idea of having a team of young, clean-cut students working their way through an education, moving their furniture. This simple name change resulted in a total image change in the mind of the public. Your name can actually be a positioning statement for your business.

The KISS principle

In trying to dream up imaginative names, it is important not to try to be *too* clever. You could end up losing the plot entirely and finish up with a name that is difficult to remember and has absolutely nothing to do with the type of business you are in. Personally, I am a great believer in the old philosophy of Keep It Simple Sweetheart (the KISS principle) when it comes to the choice of a business name. While it can be great fun to be creative and try to come up with a name that really gets people talking about you, often the simplest things work the best.

In trying to think of a suitable name, try bearing in mind three basic thoughts and see if you can't incorporate them into your business name. They are:

- *Who you are*
- *Where you are, and*
- *What you do*

The simple combination of where you are and what you do, can bring in a powerful amount of extra business. For instance, if you had a friend in the Bankstown District Hospital and you wanted to send them some flowers in a hurry, chances are you would look in the telephone book under the name Bankstown Florist. The people in this industry are quick to recognise the impact of geographical identification and such names are highly sought after and are often worth quite a bit of money in their own right.

A classic example of how this type of business name can be effective was brought home to me recently when I had some overseas visitors staying with me. We were looking for somewhere to go for dinner and I wanted to show them a little bit of the culture of Sydney but time was at a premium. I remembered there was an excellent seafood take-away cafe, right opposite Bronte beach not far from my place, where you could buy a superb fish and chip dinner and then take your meal down to the beach and watch the sun setting over the surf. But was it open and could I order ahead to save a long wait in the queue?

I couldn't remember the name of the place but a quick look in the Sydney white page telephone directory revealed the name *Bronte Seafoods.* A brief telephone call confirmed that they were open for business and I could order ahead. The point here is, had they been called *Fred's Fabulous Fish Cafe,* they wouldn't have got my business. Some time later I tried to contact this same establishment again but could no longer find them in the telephone book. I later discovered they had changed their name to something they thought was much more original. I still can't remember what it is!

A word of warning: There is a down side to names that incorporate their location, particularly where the name of the suburb is used. What happens if the business wants to expand to other areas? You need to assess the value of having the location in the name and the likelihood of your expansion before you start in business. We are all aware of businesses that carry a suburban name that is different from the suburb they are in. Do you need to take the name with you? If Bronte Seafoods opened a branch in Bondi for instance, maybe they could call their new outlet Bondi Seafoods, however chances are the name would already be taken and they would also lose the advantages to be gained by promoting the two outlets under the same name, i.e. *Fred's Fabulous Fish Cafe* - now at two great locations, Bronte and Bondi!

Beware, although it may seem like a remote possibility at the time of starting out, you could surprise yourself *(and your mother in law!)* by expanding your business well beyond your wildest dreams.

A classic example (on a much larger scale) of a business that outgrew its name is *Westpac Banking.* Those of us old enough to remember will recall it used to be called *The Bank of New South Wales*. It must have been a tough decision for Australia's oldest free enterprise bank to change its name but the name was totally inappropriate for a business that now trades all over Australia as well as in many other parts of the world.

Checklist for business names
Here are some tips for selecting a business name from a good friend of mine, Leo Fuller-Quinn, who has spent virtually a lifetime in advertising:

• Be aware of the 'look' of the name, i.e., how will it look on a sign, will it look good on your letterhead and business card - will it fit - is it too long? Use the KISS principle and keep it simple. Remember, KISS can also stand for - *Keep It Short and Sweet!*

• Is is spelt phonetically? In other words, do you write it down exactly as you say it? Some large companies spend a fortune teaching people how to say their name, for example Hyundai (pronounced *he-un-day*), Sony (pronounced *sew - nee* not sunny), and there are all sorts of names that are difficult to pronounce, let alone spell and consequently are even more difficult to remember.

• What does the name *'sound'* like? Will it work on radio and by word of mouth? Is it a name that is easy to remember and therefore easy to pass on to friends? Or will people spend much of their time saying, "They're a great company to deal with, wish I could remember their name!" Will you spend the next half of your life repeating and spelling your name on the telephone?
One of my pet hates is business names that have capital letters in the middle of a word, like *TectroDatA*. These types of names seem to be increasingly popular lately with computer companies for some strange reason. They might be in vogue at the moment but personally, I think they only serve to confuse people.

• Be sure you understand the full meaning of your chosen name. Look it up in the Oxford Dictionary; you may find it has a totally different meaning and connotation to what you thought.

• And finally, leave your personal and business ego behind when creating a name. For instance, you could spend years building up a business under your own personal name and then find this makes it very difficult to sell the business to somebody else in the future. Base your business name on what your customers are looking for and their needs, not subjective claims and boasts about your product or service.

Summary

Once you have established the name you wish to use, next you must ascertain whether the name is available for use or if somebody else is already using the name or a very similar one that will prevent you from registering it. Recent changes to the business names registration laws now allow you to use names that are similar to existing ones, unlike the old Act, however, this does not mean that you can try to pass yourself off as some other business with a well established name, even if you are allowed to register it.

The owner of a business name is entitled to take legal action to prevent you from using your name, if it can be proved that you are deliberately trying to pass yourself off as them and thus gain some form of commercial advantage by deceit.

Be warned: most companies are very jealous of their name and will sue vigorously if they perceive any threat. It simply isn't worth the risk.

To register a business name, you will need to visit the Business Names section of the Corporate Affairs Commission in your state or territory. There you can search their records to see if anyone else has already registered it. Be warned: certain types of names are forbidden from use, such as names that could be passed off as a government department or charitable institution, etc.

So, go to it; put on your thinking cap and start working on a name of your business. Give it a good deal of thought because once you have chosen your name, chances are you will be stuck with it for a long time to come.

25. CUSTOMER SERVICE

"Your customers don't care how much you know, until they know how much you care."
Gerhard Gschwandtner

One of the big advantages small businesses have over their larger counterparts is their ability to provide personalised customer service. How many times have you been into a shop which is part of a large chain organisation and been treated with indifference or even quite rudely? Most of us have a story to tell about such experiences.

The good news for the small business operator is, because you are much closer to the coal face you are generally in a position to offer a better all-round service. Also, when you own the business you are more likely to care. This is often overlooked or simply taken for granted; however, used to its full advantage, it can be a powerful weapon in your battle to win customers.

The truth is, people care a lot more about the standard of service you give them than they let on. For instance, a research company recently surveyed over 1,000 customers of a large restaurant chain to find out why they didn't come back. Their findings would probably surprise you. Only 18 per cent of those surveyed said they didn't return because of dissatisfaction with the food. Less than 20 per cent said they didn't return because of poor decor or atmosphere. However, a massive 68 per cent said they didn't return because of poor quality service! Service is the thing that keeps customers coming back to your business, time after time.

It has been estimated that it costs five times as much to get a new customer as it does to retain an existing one. Therefore, it makes good sense to ensure that once you establish a customer, they will continue to buy from you. And if they become happy customers, they will not only give you their repeat business they will also tell all their friends about you. And the way to get them talking about you is to offer more than expected. After all, if you went into a shop to make a purchase and you received pleasant and courteous service, you would be satisfied. You would have got what you expected, right? Nothing more and nothing less. The service would be considered *good* but *ordinary*. When was the last time a friend said to you, "You must go down to XYZ & Company, I can really recommend them, their service is so ordinary". *See what I mean?*

Little things mean a lot
The difference between ordinary service and extraordinary service is that little bit *extra*. You need to find a way to make your customers remember you. And make no mistake about it, despite all the emphasis being placed on customer service these days, good service is still something of a rarity and outstanding service is exceedingly rare so, to stand out from the pack, all you have to do is try that little bit harder.

Australian Airlines recently introduced a policy where the flight crew in first and business class are given a computer printout before the flight listing the passengers' names. Imagine how I felt when the flight attendant came up to me and smiled and said, "Would you like another cup of coffee, Mr. Thorpe?"

On my last flight from Melbourne to Sydney on Australian Airlines, I counted up the number of times the hostess called me by my name - *it was no less than four times!* I was impressed. Customers (like most people) just love to hear the sound of their own name.

A classic example of the power of this type of thing at work is the story of Rick the doorman at a large Adelaide hotel. Rick is no ordinary doorman. He has an uncanny ability to remember people and their names. How would you feel if when checking into your hotel, you were greeted at the door by a smiling Rick who not only remembers your name but when you were last at the hotel.

"Good morning Mr. Johnson, welcome back to the hotel. We haven't seen you for a while, must be at least ten months?" More often than not he's dead right. Extraordinary!

Does this little personal touch pay off? Barry Urquart, author of the book *Serves You Right* and a customer service expert says, when asked where they wanted to stay, the entire Queensland Grand Prix organising team simply said, "We don't care which hotel you book us into as long as it's the one where Rick is the doorman"! Powerful stuff from such an apparently *'small'* thing!

Lifetime customer value

In trying to develop a customer service attitude and culture in your business, try to think of your customers in terms of their *Lifetime Customer Value (LCV)*. Don't think of your clients or customers on a short-term basis, such as how much they will spend with you in the next week or month. Try to think of them in terms of their potential spending power if they continued to use your business over and over again for the rest of their life.

For instance, imagine you own a restaurant and a customer comes in with his friend for dinner and spends $50. If he never comes back you have gained $50 turnover and that's that. But imagine if that customer enjoyed your food and service and came back once a week for a whole year. You have gained $2,600. Imagine if he did the same thing for the next twenty years. That's a staggering $52,000 in potential turnover. Conversely, if that customer is unhappy and you lose him, you are not losing $50, you are losing potentially more than 1,000 times that amount!

In his book *Customers for Life,* car dealer Carl Sewell estimates that during their lifetime a customer is worth around $332,000 to his business. If you started thinking about each one of your customers in terms of their LCV it puts a whole new perspective on customer service.

Lee Fowler, a good friend and well known trainer who specialises in customer service, says the best way to establish what your customers want is to start out by asking them. Sounds simple doesn't it but very few businesses bother to do it. You can get them to fill in a questionnaire or you can ask them individually or in focus groups. Lee says most customers are only too happy to cooperate and are usually delighted that you care enough about them to ask.

Once you have found out what they want, make sure you implement a plan to deliver it and make sure the customers know about the changes in your service and keep coming back to test you out.

The power of delivering excellent customer service cannot be stressed too highly. If you can come up with the goods in this area, you are well on your way down the road to success.

26. NETWORKING

"He who whispers down the well,
about the products he has to sell,
doesn't gather the amount of dollars,
as he who climbs the tree and hollers."
Anon

One of the best and cheapest ways of spreading the news about your business is by networking. While the word *'networking'* became a buzz word in the 1980s, it simply means making contacts with other people and using those people to help you in your business, and there is definitely nothing new about that!

Unfortunately, some people feel uncomfortable about this prospect and think that using people to get what you want is a bit tacky. However, if you approach it on the basis of offering to help other people in return for them helping you, it is a win/win situation and perfectly healthy. There's an old saying that goes: "help enough people to get what *they* want and you will get what *you* want".

There are many ways you can extend your circle of contacts. It could be as simple as joining a community based group such as Rotary, Lions, Apex or Toastmasters. Then there are special interest groups like SWAP (Salespeople with a Purpose) and the Entrepreneurs Network. There are also groups like the Australia-Japan Society and the American Chamber of Commerce and several large women's groups. Joining your local Chamber of Commerce is another good way of meeting like-minded people. You could also join your local church group. Even if you are not a terribly religious person, it is still a good way of meeting people and who knows, you may get converted?

157

Attending seminars and courses is yet another good way of meeting people. Good networkers are constantly on the lookout for groups and *'clusters'* of people, where one contact can lead to another. Ethnic groups for instance, usually build strong support networks and if you can get involved in some of these you can rest assured it will be a big help to your business.

How to network

The secret of good networking lies in being prepared to give out a lot more than you get back. If you adopt this attitude, you will probably be surprised at how soon the scales tip in your favour and how much you are getting back. If you try to join a network by simply taking all you can get and never offering anything in return, you will soon be recognised as a 'taker' not a 'giver' and you will not last too long in the group. A strong network can be very supportive, just like a family, and can also provide a great sounding board for ideas and opportunities.

One of the greatest networkers I have ever known is my good friend and mentor John Nevin, former managing director of World Book Encyclopaedia. In all the years I have known him, he has never forgotten to call me or send me a card on my birthday, even though I am ashamed to say I have often forgotten his. John sends me notes from all over the world. They are always interesting and usually contain a newspaper clipping or some small item of particular interest to me. The amazing thing about this man is, I know literally dozens of people who also receive letters or notes from him, which invariably contain some item of particular interest to them. They are not just *newsy* type letters that have been copied and sent to a number of different people, they are always personalised in some way. Herein lies the secret of being a good networker: *to build a good network you need to build up personal relationships with people*. One of the best ways to do this is to find out what their special interests are and then use that as your common bond.

A lot of people (some of whom should know better) still think that networking is simply a matter of exchanging business cards. I would call this more pot luck. I have been to numerous seminars and handed out hundreds of business cards and collected the same amount. Usually nothing much happens unless you are lucky

158

enough to strike somebody who just happens to have an immediate need for your product or service.

Let me give you an example of how you could network and build a personal relationship:

Supposing you met somebody at a business meeting and you wanted to establish an ongoing contact with that person. Let's say that during your discussions with that person you discovered one of their hobbies was collecting bonsai plants. You later read in your local newspaper that an expert on bonsai is going to be visiting Australia soon and is holding a public seminar. Imagine the impact if you dropped this person a brief note saying something like this:

> *Hello again Jane,*
>
> *It was great meeting with you the other day. By the way, I was fascinated to hear that you collect bonsai plants. I saw this item in the local paper and thought that it might be of interest to you.*
>
> *I enjoyed talking with you and I hope we meet again soon.*
>
> *Regards,*
> *Peter*

You would be amazed at how powerful this type of contact can be. People are impressed that you have not only remembered them but their interest too and actually gone out of your way to help them. Of course, this type of approach is only for the serious networker, as it takes a lot of time and effort. It is also a great help if you are a sincere person and genuinely like helping others.

If you don't have the time or the inclination to adopt this sort of approach, you could try a more direct method. I recently attended an Amcham (American Chamber of Commerce) luncheon and did the traditional card swapping ceremony with somebody I met during the pre-dinner cocktails. It was a very short meeting as I moved around the room trying to meet as many people as I could. A few days later this letter arrived out of the blue:

Dear Peter,

It was a fleeting hello at Friday's Amcham luncheon but having secured your business card, I am doing the proverbial networking and enclosed are my current rates for temporary and permanent staff.

Please do not hesitate to call me if I can be of assistance in any of your staffing needs. I am also enclosing a blurb on Crew Find just for interest.

Regards,
Linda Williams
Career Blazers

"Not bad", I thought. It was an open and refreshingly honest approach. It was certainly a good follow up and a vast improvement on just exchanging a business card which would probably have ended up being filed in my *'round filing cabinet'*! No doubt you will be able to come up with a few ideas and variations of your own.

Summary

So, now that you've got the general idea, go forth and network and watch your business grow. After all, if you did need something, you would rather buy it from a friend or a friendly contact, wouldn't you? And by the way, one final note of warning: *don't expect to get overnight results*. Good relationships are built over a long period of time and networking is a lifetime occupation, not a short-term project.

SECTION FOUR:

BUSINESS
PLANNING

27. HOW TO CALCULATE PROFIT MARGINS

"Business without profit is not business; anymore than a pickle is a candy."
Charles Abbott

If you are buying or manufacturing goods for re-sale, in order to estimate your cash flow and budget projections, it is vital that you understand how to work out your exact profit margin. This can be done in two ways: either as a *mark up* on cost or as a *gross profit margin* based on your selling price.

Mark up
Mark up is the amount of profit you make on the *cost price* of the goods. This is arrived at by dividing the difference between the cost price and the selling price *(the gross profit)* by the cost price.
For instance:

A. Selling price of merchandise	$15.00
B. Buying price (cost) of merchandise	$10.00
Difference (A - B) =	$ 5.00

In the example above, the gross profit is $5.00. This is the amount of profit made before allowing for any expenses or overheads.

Now, divide the gross profit by the cost price and then multiply the answer by 100 to get the percentage of markup, as follows:

$5 \div 10 = 0.5 \times 100 = 50$

Your *markup* is therefore 50 per cent.

Take a calculator and complete the following exercises:
(answers at the end of this chapter plus the methods used)

Exercise 1:

Calculate the percentage of markup if we buy an item at $50.00 and sell it for $70.00.

selling price	$70.00
buying price	$50.00
gross profit =	$20.00

What is your markup on cost, expressed as a percentage?

Answer.............................%

Exercise 2:

Calculate the markup percentage on the following:

A. Buying price $120 selling price $150

Answer.............................% markup

B. Buying price .60 cents selling price $1

Answer.............................% markup

C. Selling price $75 buying price $40

Answer................................% markup

D. Selling price $9.95 buying price $5

Answer................................% markup

To calculate your selling price with a margin added at a fixed percentage, you multiply your buying price by 1. *(one point)* and the number of the percentage. For instance, if the markup you want to achieve is 40 per cent on cost, you would multiply your cost price by 1.40.

e.g. Cost price $60 X 1.40 = 84. Therefore your selling price of an item that cost you $60.00 would need to be $84 if you wanted to achieve a markup of 40 per cent.

If your percentage markup on cost was 25 per cent you would multiply the cost price by 1.25

e.g. Cost price $40 X 1.25 = $50.

Exercise 3:

Let's say your markup was 20 per cent and your cost price was $60, what would your selling price be?

(60.00 X 1.20 =)

Answer $................................

Gross profit percentages

Now, let's look at gross profit margin or GP as it is more commonly known. You can calculate your gross profit margin in much the same way as the example above, except that this time you divide your margin by the selling price (instead of the buying price) and then multiply it by 100.

For instance, if the selling price was $15.00 and the buying price was $10.00, here is how you would calculate your gross profit margin, as a percentage:

Selling price	$15.00
Buying price	$10.00
	======
gross profit (difference)	$ 5.00

$5.00 \div 15.00 = .333 \times 100 = 33.33$

Therefore, our gross profit margin (before any operating expenses have been deducted) is 33.33 per cent.

So, in the above example, our *markup* is 50 per cent and our gross profit is 33.33 per cent.

Exercise 4:

Work out the gross profit as a percentage on the following:

A. Selling price $1,250 cost price $800

Answer.................................%

B. Cost price $72 selling price $100

Answer.............................%

C. Selling price $25,000 cost price $20,000

Answer.............................%

D. Cost price $12.00 selling price $18.00

Answer.............................%

167

In many businesses the gross profit varies from item to item. In such cases you can calculate your average gross profit by taking the entire turnover for a period and doing the same calculation.

Example:

Weekly turnover in Eric's Electrical Shop is $8,000. His total cost of the goods is $6,000, therefore his total gross profit in dollar terms is $2,000. Divide this amount by the total turnover figure and multiply it by 100 to get your average gross profit percentage, as follows:

$2,000 \div 8,000 = 0.25 \times 100 = 25.$

His gross profit margin on sales is therefore 25 per cent.

To calculate the gross profit (in dollars), we just multiply the turnover amount by the percentage, as follows:

Let's say our gross profit was 25 per cent and our turnover was $10,000. To find out what that is in dollar terms, we would multiply the turnover figure of $10,000 by .25 (point 25)

$10,000 \times .25 = 2,500$

Therefore, if our gross profit is 25 per cent and our turnover is $10,000, we will make $2,500 gross profit.

Exercise 5:

A. If our turnover was $22,450 what would our gross profit be if we were making an average of 33.3 per cent gross profit on turnover?

Answer = $..............................

B. If our turnover was $310,500 and our gross profit margin was 37% what would our gross profit be?

Answer = $..............................

Now that we have learnt how to calculate markup and gross margin, let's put that to use in some real-life scenarios:

Exercise 6:

A. Jan wants to start a small gift shop in the local shopping centre. She has calculated that her total expenses per week, allowing for wages, rent and other costs, are $2,400. She estimates her turnover per week (based on her market research and estimated traffic flow through the centre) will be $6,000 per week.
Her average gross profit margin (based on industry standards) is estimated to be 40 per cent. How much profit will she make after allowing for all her costs?

Answer = $.............................

B. If she managed to achieve an average gross profit margin of 55 per cent on her turnover of $6,000 a week, how much net profit would she make? (Allow for the same total expenses of $2,400).

Answer = $..

N.B. Any extra profit earned would probably be subject to additional variable expenses (refer to notes on variable expenses in budgeting section).

C. Joe turns over $12,000 a week in his spare parts business. His average gross profit is 35 per cent. His total expenses are $2,700 a week. How much is his net profit per week?

Answer = $.............................

ANSWERS:

exercise 1: 40%
exercise 2: A. 25% B. 66% C. 87.5% D. 99%
exercise 3: $72
exercise 4: A. 36% B. 28% C, 20% D. 33.3%
exercise 5: A. $7,475.85 B. $114,885
exercise 6: A. nil B. $900 C. $1,500

HOW THE ANSWERS WERE CALCULATED:

exercise 1
20 ÷ 50 = .4 X 100 = 40

exercise 2:
A. 150 - 120 = 30 ÷ 120 = .25 X 100 = 25
B. 1.00 - .60 = .40 ÷ .60 = .66 X 100 = 66
C. 75 - 40 = 35 ÷ 40 = .87.5 X 100 = 87.5
D. 9.95 - 5.00 = 4.95 ÷ 5.00 = .99 X 100 = 99

exercise 3:
60.00 X 1.20 = 72.

exercise 4:
A. 1,250 - 800 = 450 ÷ 1.250 = .36 X 100 = 36
B. 100 - 72 = 28 ÷ 100 = .28 X 100 = 28
C. 25,000 - 20,000 = 5,000 ÷ 25,000 = .2 X 100 = 20
D. 18 - 12 = 6 ÷ 18 = .3333 X 100 = 33.33

exercise 5:
A. 22,450 X .333 = 7,475.85
B. 310,500 X .37 = 114,885

exercise 6:
A. 6,000 X .40 = 2,400 - 2,400 = NIL
B. 6,000 X .55 = 3,300 - 2,400 = 900
C. 12,000 X .35 = 4,200 - 2,700 = 1,500

28. PRICING FOR PROFIT

*"Service and quality will be remembered long after
price is forgotten."*
Anon.

One of the biggest mistakes many small business owners make is underpricing their goods or services. Too many small operators place far too much emphasis on price, often quite unnecessarily. Sadly, many of them don't get their price for one simple reason: *they are afraid to ask for it!*

Many think just because they are smaller, they have to be drastically cheaper than the big guys. In actual fact small businesses, because of their flexibility and ability to adapt to market conditions and requirements more quickly, can often justify charging as much or even more than their big business counterparts. Most people are quite happy to pay more for better, quicker or more personalised service. Too few small business people realise this and many a small operator has gone broke through cutting prices to an unrealistic level.

And it's not just small businesses that get into trouble with price cutting. Take the case of Bob Ansett's Budget car rental business and more recently Compass Airlines. The receiver manager of Compass Airlines at one stage estimated that the difference between going broke and making a profit was as little as $9 per seat, per journey. When you consider that at the height of the airline fare wars, some journeys were slashed by hundreds of dollars, this seems ridiculous. After Compass went into receivership, thousands of people rallied to their support and said they wished they had used their services more often. What a pity they had to go broke to prove to their potential market how important they were!

Of course, there are various other reasons why Compass got into

171

financial difficulty but certainly the prime one was cutting their prices and margins to a point below that at which the company could operate profitably.

A word of warning here: be very careful about starting a business based purely on being able to supply a product or service at a cheaper price than your competitors. While it may be relatively easy to grab a slice of the market by offering the cheapest prices, the secret lies in being able to do this effectively and still manage to stay in business in the long term. Most businesses have common overheads and fixed costs, so sooner or later businesses that sell on price alone generally come unstuck. Another common mistake with pricing is failing to understand the real cost of operating the business, usually caused through poor record keeping. Of course, there are exceptions to every rule. Some business operators have been able to build themselves huge markets by undercutting the opposition and offering a *'no frills'* alternative.

Unfortunately all too often, cutting the price is seen as the answer to the problem of flagging sales but it can actually serve to inflame the problem. Let's take a look at the drastic effect (on the bottom line) of even a 10 per cent drop in the selling price by a typical business:

	before discount ($)	after discount ($)
Sales:		
2,000 units at $1,000 each	2,000,000	
2,000 units at $900 each		1,800,000
less cost of goods:		
2,000 units at $800 each	1,600,000	1,600,000
gross profit	400,000	200,000
less sales expenses and overheads	300,000	300,000
net profit or (loss) before tax	100,000	(100,000) *loss*

172

That example shows what happens when prices are dropped by even a relatively modest ten per cent to maintain a market share. This assumes that the volume of sales remains the same as before the price cutting exercise and doesn't increase or decrease.

Now, let's see what happens if we don't drop the price and as a direct result of this our turnover drops by 20 per cent:

Sales: (20% less than previous)

1,600 units at $1,000 each	1,600,000
less cost of goods:	
1,600 units at $800 each	1,280,000
	========
gross profit	320,000
less expenses and overheads	300,000 *
	========
net profit before tax	20,000

You can see from the above exercise, we can sustain a massive 20 per cent drop in sales and still make a modest profit (as opposed to a $100,000 loss if we drop our selling price by 10 per cent). Imagine the effect on our bottom line in the first scenario if we cut our selling price by 10 per cent and still suffer a 20 per cent drop in sales! This is quite feasible, especially if the reason we are losing market share is not simply price but other factors.

* Note: In actual fact we would probably reduce some of the variable content of the sales expenses and overheads, thereby increasing the profit situation even further. For instance, we could have fewer telephone calls, use less petrol delivering goods and we might even be able to get by with fewer staff members and/or smaller premises, etc. Some of the overheads such as the rent, etc. may be fixed, regardless of the sales volume but the variable overheads will generally reduce.

Before deciding on your selling prices, check that your margins are in line with normal industry standards. These figures are usually available from industry associations and trade organisations or the Australian Bureau of Statistics. You may be able to get a profile of your industry from the Financial Management Research Centre at Armidale, NSW, telephone (067) 725 199.

If your prices are uncompetitive and you are finding it difficult to compete, go back and recheck your overheads and buying prices. Maybe you are overstaffed, paying too much for premises or not buying well enough or it may be a combination of all these things.

How to overcome price cutting
So, if you are in a very price competitive industry, how do you overcome the problem?

Very often the answer lies in providing better customer service or by simply being quicker, more efficient, having more product knowledge, etc. This is known as *adding value*. Let me give you an example: I recently wanted to buy a second hand car for my wife. What I know about the workings of motor cars could be written on the back of a postage stamp! I know there's an engine under the bonnet somewhere and that's about it.

I wanted to buy the car privately to save money but I had no idea of what to look out for. The logical step for me to take was to get some professional help. I rang a large motorists' association and inquired about the cost of a vehicle check. The price seemed quite reasonable but when I went to make a booking, they couldn't come for two days. Nor could they give me an approximate time of arrival, which meant that I would need to wait in, perhaps all day. Of course, this was not suitable. If you are buying a secondhand car you need to be quick off the mark. Most sellers won't wait two days for you to get a second opinion!

I noticed in the 'cars for sale' columns of the newspapers, there were a number of other smaller companies advertising what appeared to be a similar service. I decided to call some and check them out. Their price was around the same as the larger organisation and one company was even quite a bit dearer. The big difference was in the service they provided. If I wanted to go ahead, they told me, they could have their man there *within the hour!*

I decided to give them a go and they were true to their word. The man was there within an hour of my telephone call and he provided what turned out to be a very satisfactory service. Whether it was as good or better than the service provided by the big organisation, I will never know. The point is they were providing a service suitable for the job at hand at a time and place to suit me, the customer, not them. In other words they were catering to the customer's needs, not *their* needs! Price was to a large extent secondary. Service was the key issue in this case.

Naturally, when all things are equal, most people will tend to buy from the larger, well known organisation with the backing of a big name. Your task is to find ways of giving your business the leading edge. Quite often large companies can be totally inflexible. I had a similar experience when I was getting my swimming pool installed. I had to get some soil removed and needed several large waste bins. I rang a big, well known company with a large ad in the yellow pages. They could deliver the bins, they said but they couldn't give me a time for the replacement bin (when the first one was full). This meant the workmen would be standing around waiting, perhaps for hours. Once again, a small local firm came to my rescue. All I had to do was telephone them when each bin was nearly full and they would send somebody around straight away with a fresh one.

There are many examples of just how inflexible some large companies can be. In fact, it makes you wonder sometimes how some big firms ever get to be *big* in the first place!

What do your customers really want?

It probably sounds ridiculous but very often customers don't really know what it is they want to buy! For this reason, price is often less important in making a sale than you might think. A friend of mine Martin Grunstein, was doing some work with a travel group. They were continually losing sales to people who rang up or called in and asked questions such as, "What's your best price on a return airfare to London?"

In such cases the sales assistants normally quoted a price and that was usually the last they saw or heard of the inquirer. Martin did some research and discovered that very few people wanted to simply fly to London and back. More often than not, this was simply a starting out point for people wishing to travel overseas but not wanting to show their lack of knowledge. They didn't want to walk into a travel agency and say, "I'd like to travel overseas but I don't really know much about it!"

By training their sales people in a simple questioning technique, Martin was able to show them how to find out exactly what the customer *really* wanted. Here is a typical example:

Customer: "How much is your cheapest return airfare to London?"
Sales consultant: *"When did you wish to travel?"*
Customer: "Probably in the summer holidays."
Sales consultant: *"Have you been to London before, sir?"*
Customer: "No."
Sales consultant: *"And how many people will be travelling?"*
Customer: "My wife, myself and two children."
Sales consultant: *"How long did you plan on being away?"*
Customer: "Oh, probably about three weeks."
Sales consultant: *"How many stopovers did you wish to make?"*
Customer: "Well, we hadn't really thought about that yet."
Sales consultant: *"Well, have you ever thought about going via Hawaii and the United States. I'll bet the kids would love to see Disneyland and it may not cost that much more. In fact, at the moment we have a special package, etc. etc..."*

You can see how a simple questioning technique can break down the barriers and reveal a customer's true wants and needs. It is important when using this type of technique that the questions are asked in a friendly and non-threatening way. You must show a genuine interest and a desire to help. The questions should be seen as assisting the client to get what he or she wants, not just to give them the runaround. People who are simply interested in the best price soon get irritated by the questioning technique, cut the conversation short and move on to the next travel agent and the next, until they find the rock bottom price. If you build your business around these sorts of customers (who care only about price and nothing about service), you won't have much of a business and you are probably better off without them.

176

Summary

Service and *flexibility* are your two major weapons in the battle to compete with the big firms. Be constantly aware of them. Big armies usually beat small armies, so you have to resort to guerrilla warfare. You must seek out your enemy's weak points and utilise your strong points to their best advantage. Big companies have it all over you when it comes to resources and buying power but often it's the little things that make the difference. Find out what your market really wants. Is there some additional service or benefit you can offer that will give you the leading edge and make people want to deal with you?

Talk to your clients and potential clients. More importantly, listen to what they are saying. Ask questions. As the Americans would say, find out where their *hot button* is and *what turns them on*. Chances are you can come up with something that will give your business the leading edge.

29. WHAT FINANCIERS WANT

"Capital can do nothing without the brains to direct it."
J. Ogden Armour

The events of the late eighties and early nineties radically changed the attitudes and approaches of financiers. Until the switch, the aggressive market of banking deregulation placed the emphasis on competing with foreign banks and on protecting market share. This bullish approach by lenders rewarded managers for growth. The catch phrase for the period was, *lend, lend, lend* - and with hindsight - *at any cost!*

When the real cost of that expansionist era was evaluated, it became clear that not enough emphasis had been placed on the assessment of risk and thorough evaluation of loan applications. Loan approval procedures have since been rigorously reviewed and loan criteria now concentrates more on the financier's bottom line. Business needs to adapt to this new environment. Primarily, financiers lend to *people* not to *ideas*. This climate means that professional submissions to raise finance are now more essential than ever. Borrowers must demonstrate that they have what financiers call the 5 'Cs'. This stands for capital, *character, capacity* and *collateral* and *conditions*.

Capital
This simply refers to the amount of money you want to borrow and how long you want it for.

Character

This refers to the personal integrity and reputation of the people behind the business. Have you got a good personal track record? Are there any financial 'skeletons' in your closet? If you have had credit problems in the past, it is probably better to come clean and talk about them up front because chances are they are going to be discovered in due course.

Capacity

Next, financiers will be looking closely at your *capacity* to repay the loan. This doesn't just mean *service* the loan by repaying the interest. These days financiers are looking for the capacity, management ability and commitment to service the interest, repay the capital and generate a return to your business. A finance proposal should be integrated with a business plan to demonstrate that an organisation is a good lending opportunity.

Collateral

And finally, *collateral*. What assets do you have that can be called on if you fail to meet your commitment? While financiers will be looking for security, the viability of the business will be the primary consideration; the security issues follow.

Banks will usually only move on your assets when all other means of collecting have been exhausted. In the eyes of a bank, if they have to take this action, they would view it as a bad lending decision in the first place.

Conditions

The final consideration will be given to the conditions of the market at the time. Is it growing or declining? Is it likely to be affected by any outside factors or influences?

To evaluate what is a *good lending opportunity* for financiers, and the new approach to lending in the nineties, Ernst & Young undertook a survey of the four major trading banks and other banks in the market.*

What follows is a brief summary of their findings:

179

Attitudes and approaches

Many emerging businesses feel that financiers have overcompensated for previous bad loans and are now too conservative in their lending approach. Financiers of course, still want to lend. The Ernst & Young survey however, revealed that financiers generally feel that business owners need to change their attitude to the retention of cash in their business.

In the past, lifestyle considerations have all too often eclipsed the need to build profit and cash reserves. In many instances, no distinctions were made between personal money and business money. Investments in 'ego', rather than recognition of the need to preserve cash, were common in many businesses.

Repayment

In terms of the lending policy of the nineties, the key word is *repayment*.

In the years prior to the current more conservative approach to lending, financiers looked at the serviceability of a loan. Today, it is not good enough to receive interest only. The borrower's exit strategy must be presented. In other words, lenders want to know how and when the money is likely to be repaid in full. The onus is now firmly on the borrower to create an individually strong lending case. With the loan approval process becoming more comprehensive and stringent, the emphasis for financiers is on clever credit assessment.

What financiers want

First and foremost, financiers do want to lend to business. They are in business to lend money and business is an important market segment. Ernst & Young's survey found that financiers' key expectations of business were that they:

- *demonstrate sound management skills*
- *provide accurate financial data*
- *provide regular and timely financial data*
- *prepare cash flow projections with substance, and*
- *demonstrate capacity to pay interest and repay capital.*

Financiers strongly indicated that the above expectations are currently not being satisfied and this has created major problems with business lending facilities.

The survey also found that financiers:

- *favour a professional presentation and an accounting firm's involvement in the provision of frequent financial reporting*
- *expect that such advisers should have made the client aware of any weakness in their finance submission prior to its presentation to the financier*
- *prefer businesses to obtain all finance from the one source*
- *prefer to see a reduction in the number of trust structures*
- *prefer businesses to be audited.*

Summary

Banks in the nineties are placing a greater emphasis on *'relationship banking'* – getting close to their customers, getting to know the business and the character of the people who run the business. They want to see sound business management demonstrated. Evaluation of lending proposals today concentrate on management capabilities and the viability of a business, including capital structures and industry type. Security is considered *after* the proposals pass this stage. Financiers are no longer simply security lenders; at the same time they will not lend *without* security.

Financiers are looking for more discipline within businesses and a move away from tax-driven structures and modes of operation. For businesses to connect with the financiers' lending objectives, it is essential that they are aware of what financiers want.

* The report "Business Financial Strategies" was prepared by the Business Services Group of Ernst & Young. The author wishes to thank them for their assistance in preparing this chapter.

30. PROJECTING YOUR CASH FLOW

"Happiness is a positive cash flow."
Fred Adler

The financial part of your business plan will need to include a cash flow projection. This simply means a forecast of the amount of money that will be flowing in and out of your business. Many small businesses get into trouble through poor control of cash flow or underestimation of their capital requirements.

To maintain a healthy cash flow, you need to have tight control over your operating expenses and overheads (both fixed and variable), your level of stock, your collection of debts and your profitability. The best way to control these factors is to budget for them and constantly monitor the results.

Capital requirements
Whether you buy an existing business or startup from scratch, you will require a certain amount of *startup capital*. You will also need money to run the business and pay wages, which is called *working capital*. How much working capital you will need is a bit like asking *"how long is a piece of string?"* It depends on many different factors but as a guide, I would recommend enough to carry you through from three to six months with no money coming in at all.

Small busines capital usually comes in two major forms:

- *Your own funds (or your partner's) that you invest in the business, which is called equity capital, and*
- *Money you borrow from others, which is called debt capital.*

It is highly desirable to keep the amount of debt capital to a minimum, otherwise you may find the cost of servicing the debt drains all the profit from the business and eventually sends you broke. Businesses with borrowings far higher than their equity capital are said to be *highly geared* or in the case of very high borrowings, *over geared*. This is highly dangerous and should be avoided. Once again, it is difficult to say what an acceptable ratio of debt vs. equity capital is, but a good rule of thumb would be not to borrow more than the amount you put in.

To work out whether your business venture is financially viable and to forecast your capital requirements, you will need to develop a cash flow projection. Now, let's have look at what is needed to start drawing up a cash flow projection and a capital requirement plan:

Forecasting

To formulate your plan, you will need to estimate or at least *guesstimate* a number of figures. Predicting such things as sales and expenses is an extremely difficult task, because unless you are buying a well-established business with a long history of stable trading, most of your estimates will be based purely on supposition. Try to keep the guesswork to a minimum and do your homework thoroughly to avoid being caught short.

When drawing up a cash flow projection, it is wise to prepare a number of *'what if'* scenarios. For example, what if you have the worst possible sales and the highest possible expenses? This will give you a picture of what could happen if your sales or expense projections don't live up to your expectations.

Your cash flow and profit projections should always err on the side of caution; it is far better to be pessimistic when forecasting sales and generous when it comes to forecasting expenses. Bear in mind there is always an element of uncertainty in any business venture and Murphy's Law usually applies, *i.e. if anything can go wrong, it usually does!* This is especially true when it comes to projecting cash flows.

Although you won't be able to predict accurately down to the last cent, the main objective is to have a budget plan and be constantly aware of how you are going against it. You will probably need to revise your plan (up or down) as you go along. Don't make the mistake of preparing a cash flow plan purely to arrange finance for your business and then forgetting all about it. Your plan should be realistic and continually monitored.

You will need to know or guesstimate the following items in order to draw up your financial plan:

- *Cash receipts - income from sales or other sources - projected monthly for the first year*
- *overheads (fixed and variable expenses including salaries, etc.)*
- *loan repayments*
- *purchases - cost of goods or raw materials*
- *stock level requirements*
- *capital available*
- *setting up costs such as shop fit out and/or purchase of plant and equipment.*

The first thing we have to do is make some form of sales projection on a monthly basis. This would be drawn up from our marketing plan and should take into account such things as seasonal factors.

Expenses
Next, you must allocate an amount for every type of expense you are likely to encounter in setting up and running the business. Your business will be subject to three types of general expenses, falling broadly into the following categories:

- *setting up expenses (one-off costs, such as legal fees or in the case of buying an existing business, the purchase price)*
- *fixed expenses (such as rent on premises and wages)*
- *variable expenses (such things as freight and advertising).*

The first two items, setting up and fixed expenses, are usually fairly easy to establish. Variable expenses however, may be tied to the turnover of your business and are therefore much more difficult to establish. For instance, let's say that your product contains a large amount of freight for delivery and this is included in your selling price. This would mean the more you sell, the higher your expenses would be. On the other hand, your rent will probably remain constant no matter how much you sell (unless you are in a shopping centre where you are required to pay a percentage of your turnover).

In the case of variable expenses, you may be able to estimate them as a percentage of your sales. Let's say you were selling an item for $100 and this included an average delivery charge of $5. This would mean your freight charge is five per cent of your projected sales figure.

Using the cash flow charts

On pages 188 and 189, you will find an example of what a typical cash flow chart looks like. On pages 190 and 191, you will find a blank chart for your own use.

Warning: Do not write on the pages in the book, photocopy them so that you can use them over and over for your cash flow projections. Note: You will also find it easier to write in the columns if you enlarge the page size on the photocopier.

In the top column (1) write down the months from left to right, starting with the first month of operation. The first figure you must establish is your monthly cash receipts. This will be your total income from sales, interest or fees, etc., month by month for the first 12 months of operation. Allow for any seasonal factors, such as Christmas trading or winter vs. summer. Write your projections for revenue from sales, etc. (cash receipts) for each month across column (2).

Next, in column (3) write the cost of any goods purchased for resale (purchases). Column (4) is your gross profit. This is the difference between columns (2) and (3). Next, list your expenses and overheads, items (6) to (21).

Note: Items (6) to (9) will probably be fixed expenses and items (10) to (21) will probably be variable expenses. Write any additional item of major expense (such as commissions to sales people, etc.)

185

not listed in items (6) to (21) in the space provided in (23). Minor items can be listed under miscellaneous expenses, item (21). Item (22) allows a provision for company tax instalments. If you are going to trade as a company, you will need to make provisions for this in your second financial year of trading.

Total your expenses, items (6) to (23) and write them in column (24) total expenses. Now, subtract your total expenses (24) from your gross profit (4). This will give you your total net profit (25). Subtract any capital payments, such as money paid out for shop fittings or purchase of plant or equipment (26) to arrive at your total cash flow position for the month (28). *Draw brackets around any figures that are negative.* Subtract any repayment of loans (29) and this gives you your final monthly cash flow figure (30).

Repeat the above process in the next column for the following month, only this time you carry forward the final cash flow position (30) and add it to the net profit (25) for the next month. Extend this exercise across the page for the full twelve months. Finally, add the columns across for a total in the extreme right hand column headed TOTAL. This will give you your projected trading profit or loss for the first year's operation.

Profit and loss
Note: The gross profit figure in your projected cash flow will probably vary from the figure in your *profit and loss statement* prepared by your accountant at the end of the financial year, after taking into account such things as depreciation. This document is only a cash flow projection, not a profit and loss statement. Bear in mind, if you are going to extend credit terms on your sales, you should put that income in the month that you will get paid, not the month that you make the sale. i.e. If you are allowing 30 days from statement, allow 45 to 60 days from the date of the sale to take into account slow payers.

Summary
Repeat the cash flow projection exercise over and over with all the possible variables you can think of. Remember, at this stage it's only on paper. If the bottom line is continually negative, then you obviously need to review your projections. You either need more

sales or cheaper expenses. And remember, if you do revise your sales upwards or your expenses downwards, make sure the new figures are realistic, otherwise abandon the project and look at something else. Be honest with your projections; it's no use kidding yourself -

If you are going to go broke, it is far better you do it on paper than in real life!

Good luck, and don't forget - *Happiness is a positive cash flow!*

	CASH FLOW PROJECTION FOR			A TYPICAL BUSINESS			
1	MONTH	SEP	OCT	NOV	DEC	JAN	FEB
2	cash receipts	20,000	27,000	40,000	45,000	30,000	35,000
3	purchases	32,000	25,000	26,000	35,000	22,000	21,000
4	gross profit (2 - 3)	(12,000)	2,000	14,000	10,000	8,000	14,000
5	EXPENSES						
6	gross wages	3,500	3,500	3,500	3,500	3,500	3,500
7	rent of premises	1,500	1,500	1,500	1,500	1,500	1,500
8	lease or hire purchase	165	165	165	165	165	165
9	motor vehicle lease	550	550	550	550	550	550
10	motor vehicle expenses	250	250	250	250	250	250
11	advertising/promotion	3,000	2,000	2,000	1,000	500	2,000
12	freight/delivery	200	270	400	450	300	350
13	stationery/print/post	400	400	400	400	400	400
14	telephone/fax	290	–	–	2,000	–	–
15	travel/entertaining	100	100	100	100	1,200	100
16	accountancy/legal	3,500	–	–	–	–	–
17	petty cash	200	200	200	200	200	200
18	repairs & maintenance	–	–	400	–	–	400
19	interest on loans	225	225	225	225	225	225
20	bank charges	50	50	50	50	50	50
21	miscellaneous expenses	300	300	300	300	300	300
22	co. tax installments						
23							
24	total expenses (6 to 23)	14,230	9,510	10,040	10,690	9,140	9,990
25	net profit (4 - 24)	(26,230)	(7,510)	3,960	(690)	(1,140)	4,010
26	capital payments	(16,500)*					
27	capital introduced	60,000					
28	cash flow position	17,270	9,760	13,720	13,030	11,890	15,900
29	repayment on loans						
30	cash flow position*	17,270	9,760	13,720	13,030	11,890	15,900

.................................DATE							
MAR	APR	MAY	JUN	JUL	AUG	TOTAL	NOTES
56,000	31,000	55,000	46,000	60,000	47,000	492,000	
36,000	21,000	26,000	26,000	23,000	20,000	313,000	
20,000	10,000	29,000	20,000	37,000	27,000	179,000	
3,500	3,500	3,500	3,500	3,500	3,500	42,000	
1,500	1,500	1,500	1,500	1,500	1,500	18,000	
165	165	165	165	165	165	1,980	Fax, Photocopier
550	550	550	550	550	550	6,600	
250	250	250	250	250	250	3,000	
1,000	1,500	1,000	1,000	2,000	1,00?	18,000	
560	310	550	460	600	470	4,920	1% of sales
400	400	400	400	400	400	4,800	
2,000	–	–	2,000	–	–	6,290	
100	100	100	100	100	100	2,300	*Travel to trade fair
–	–	–	–	–	2,000	5,500	
200	200	200	200	200	200	2,400	
–	–	400	–	–	400	1,600	
225	225	225	75	75	–	2,175	
50	50	50	50	50	50	600	
300	300	300	300	300	300	3,600	
10,800	9,050	9,190	10,550	9,690	10,885	140,265	
9,200	950	19,810	9,450	27,310	16,115	38,735	
						(16,500)	*Shopfittings
25,100	26,050	45,860	35,310	62,620	68,735	68,735	*Same as last month
		(20,000)		(10,000)			
25,100	26,050	25,860	35,310	52,620	68,735	68,735	*After loan repayments

CASH FLOW PROJECTION FOR	....						
1	MONTH						
2	cash receipts						
3	purchases						
4	gross profit (2 - 3)						
5	EXPENSES						
6	gross wages						
7	rent of premises						
8	lease or hire purchase						
9	motor vehicle lease						
10	motor vehicle expenses						
11	advertising/promotion						
12	freight/delivery						
13	stationery/print/post						
14	telephone/fax						
15	travel/entertaining						
16	accountancy/legal						
17	petty cash						
18	repairs & maintenance						
19	interest on loans						
20	bank charges						
21	miscellaneous expenses						
22	co. tax installments						
23							
24	total expenses (6 to 23)						
25	net profit (4 - 24)						
26	capital payments						
27	capital introduced						
28	cash flow position						
29	repayment on loans						
30	cash flow position*						

WARNING DO NOT WRITE ON THIS PAGE. - PHOTOCOPY IT

......................................DATE							TOTAL	NOTES

31. THE BUSINESS PLAN

"No business plans to fail - they simply fail to plan!"
Anon.

Planning is your greatest weapon against failure. In this chapter we are going to deal with the process of preparing a plan for your business. While the main reason most people prepare a business plan is to raise finance, your business plan should not just be a tool for raising capital but a blueprint for your business's future. It is also a good way of checking the overall viability of your proposed business venture.

The steps presented here are intended to form the groundwork for the planning process. If you are going to use this plan to raise finance, it is a good idea to get an accountant or business adviser to go over it with you. You will find however, that going through these worksheets first will save you both time and money in preparing your final submission. It will also help you in evaluating the overall viability of your venture.

The Purpose of Planning
Imagine if you engaged a builder to build a house for you and he turned up at your block of land and started unloading bricks and building material and then turned around to you and said, *"Okay, where do you want the house?"* You wouldn't be very impressed, would you? Naturally, before he started building, you would expect to see a plan. Your business, just like your house, needs a thorough and well-constructed business plan in order to succeed.

193

Preparing a business plan to raise capital

If your business venture requires finance or additional capital, for instance a bank loan or overdraft facility, you should prepare a detailed business plan. Generally, banks and financial institutions will not even consider lending money without one. The more detail and accuracy you can project in your plan, the more chance it will have of being successful.

Raising finance for your business should not be a harrowing experience. If you do your homework properly you should be able to approach your financier with a sound business proposition that will be considered worthwhile for both parties. Remember, financial institutions make healthy profits from lending money on sound business propositions.

In the case of a business loan, the financier will be looking at your ability to service the loan and your net asset backing. These days they will also want to see some form of repayment plan for the loan as well. Your security normally takes the form of bricks and mortar (or other easily realisable assets) and financiers will usually require a mortgage or some form of charge over your assets to cover themselves in the event of your failure to meet your obligations.

It must be remembered that small business failure rates are extremely high and banks and other financial institutions are usually very cautious in their approach to lending in this area. Banks do not like the idea of selling you up, so even if you have the asset backing, if the business plan and the people behind it don't look sound there is no guarantee your application will be successful. They will more than likely reject you in your own self-interest.

It should be stressed that if you do fail in business and you cannot make arrangements to clear the debt, the bank or finance company may have no alternative but to move on your assets and you should be fully prepared to take that risk; otherwise, rethink the whole project.

Also make sure your spouse or other people involved are fully aware of the risks involved and the consequences of what can happen in the case of failure.

194

The business plan

If you are starting a new business from scratch, your business plan will need to consist of at least the following components:

A Contents page

Details of what is contained in your plan.

An executive summary

This is the first document in your business plan after the contents page but it is the last one you prepare. It should be not much longer than a page and should simply summarise what your plan entails. It is intended to give the person reading it a broad overview of what you are setting out to achieve.

The business objectives

A detailed description of your business strategy and objectives (precisely what you are going to do). In other words - *what is the business of your business?*

Product or service profile

A detailed description of the product or service you will be offering. If any machinery or equipment is involved, supply details of its state and condition.

A marketing plan

Include your marketing strategies and sales forecasts, including market analysis. Supply as much information as possible about the state of the market you are going to be entering, details of the competition, historical information detailing growth of the overall market, what area of the market you are aiming for and any advantages or disadvantages you are likely to have over your competitors. *(See chapter - Your Marketing Plan).*

A financial plan

A detailed financial plan for the business, both short-term (one year) and long-term projections (say three years). *Note: projecting beyond this is pointless, especially in a new business.*
Make sure that your forward projections are conservative, for

instance, don't just predict a 50 per cent increase each year unless you can solidly substantiate it. You are far more likely to be taken seriously if you project a modest annual increase.

List details of the capital required to both start up and run the business and a projected cash flow *(see chapter - Projecting Your Cash Flow)*. Your plan should also show exactly what the capital you want to borrow will be used for. For instance, will it be used for working capital or for the purpose of acquiring plant or machinery? Give details. Indicate what assumptions have been made in arriving at any budget figures, e.g. *assumes interest rates of ten per cent and an annual inflation rate of four per cent, etc*. It is also desirable to have a projected Profit and Loss Statement and Balance Sheet, especially if you are going to seek a substantial amount of money. These are fairly complex documents and you should seek the advice of an accountant in preparing them.

Repayment details of loan
Repayment is the key word for lending in the nineties. Financiers are no longer simply concerned with whether you can service the loan, they want to see evidence that you are going to eventually repay the loan. Your business plan should include details of how and when you will repay your loan, in other words, what is the exit strategy for the financier? Your repayment strategy should tie in with your cash flow projections. It could for instance detail regular monthly repayments of capital, reducing the loan over a period of time or it may be reduced by lump sum payments as the business grows and becomes more profitable. It is unlikely that lenders will be very interested in proposals that simply want to borrow money with no indication or plan to repay it.

Security of loans and guarantees
Outline details of any assets that are going to be used as security and any encumbrances on them. If you are going to use your home for example, supply details of any mortgages outstanding. It should be remembered that the project must demonstrate that it is viable and that the interest and capital repayments can be discharged during the normal course of the business. Once this has been established, then the financier will turn to security. Financiers generally

will not lend without adequate security and this is always assessed in a very conservative manner. Banks will normally nominate their own valuer to value your assets and their valuations will always be conservative and often as much as twenty per cent or more below what you consider to be the 'real' market value.

Personal financial status
Supply a personal financial statement of all the principals involved in the business, listing assets and liabilities and any ongoing income streams. *(see figure 1 page 198)*

Personal background
Supply personal details of the principals of the business venture including employment history and experience and qualifications. *(see figure 2 page 199)*

An organisational plan
This should outline the management structure, responsibility and accountability of office holders *(the people behind the business, what their function will be and to whom they will be accountable).* Detail the type of structure the business will operate under, e.g. company or partnership, etc. List names of the directors or principals and company secretary and location of registered office. Also (if possible) supply details of any staff you may be hiring and their particular expertise.

Financial reporting details
Supply details of the accounting procedure to be used for financial reporting. Note, these days financiers usually require periodic reporting, e.g. quarterly (rather than annual) reports, prepared by a professional.

Appendices
Any information or further details needed to back up or enlarge upon any of the above, such as brochures, market research, press clippings, competitors' advertisements, statistics, evidence of any trade or professional qualifications, etc.

figure 1.

PERSONAL FINANCIAL STATEMENT OF PRINCIPAL
(one for each director or partner in the business or jointly
for husband and wife)

name:...

ASSETS	VALUE
home	
other real estate	
cash available	
vehicles	
life insurance	
superannuation	
shares/investments	
other assets	

(A) total assetts =

LIABILITIES	VALUE
mortgage	
hire purchase	
credit accounts	
charge accounts	
taxation liabilities	
bank overdraft or loans	
any other liabilities	

(B) total liabilities =

total net worth (A - B) =

$..

The above is a true statement of my assets and liabilities
as at   /   /

signed..

figure 2.

PERSONAL BACKGROUND OF PRINCIPAL

name:

address:

telephone numbers: home   bus.
marital status:

spouse's occupation:

children and ages:

state of health:

sports and hobbies:

membership of associations
or other community groups:

educational standard achieved:

details of any trade or
professional qualifications held:

EMPLOYMENT HISTORY:
details of current employment:

previous employment history:

*Outline details of employment history, list any qualifications
or courses attended, especially any relating to the proposed
business venture. Also detail experience in any aspect of your
personal life that may be relevant to demonstrate leadership
or management skills, e.g. Secretary, local Lions Club, etc.*

Existing businesses and/or franchised businesses

If you are seeking to raise finance to purchase or extend an established business, you will need to include the following:

- *copies of the business's balance sheets and financial
  statements*
- *copies of the taxation returns and (if incorporated) company
  returns for the last five years*
- *a debtors and creditors analysis*
- *A copy of the business name registration or in the case of a
  company, a copy of the articles of association*
- *A complete listing of any stock inventory you are taking over*
- *A detailed report of any plant and equipment you will be
  acquiring*
- *Any feasibility studies or market surveys or consultant's
  reports*
- *If you are buying a franchised business, you will also need to
  supply a copy of the franchise agreement and/or disclosure
  document.*

Summary

After drafting your final plan, try to enlist the help of a friend or
relative who is experienced in this sort of thing and get them to take
a look at your overall plan. In the final analysis, your plan will be
judged on the following criteria:

- *completeness*
- *objectivity*
- *logic*
- *presentation*
- *the ability to effectively communicate your proposal.*

*Note: It is recommended that you seek professional advice from an
accountant or business adviser to go over your final plan and while
they are not cheap, a few dollars spent at this stage can save you a
fortune later on.*

And finally, all of the above probably sounds quite daunting;
however working through your business plan is often a good way of

establishing the viability of a business venture. Keep detailed records of your plan and compare it with your actual performance.

Some of the information required may seem of a highly personal nature but remember, the people lending you the money will want to know as much about you and your business as they can. The more details you supply, the more chance your application for finance will have of succeeding.

32. YOUR MARKETING PLAN

"Marketing is simply sales with a college education."
John Freund

People often confuse marketing with sales, as the quotation above would suggest, however while the two are closely related and one leads to the other, there are very distinct differences. Marketing is probably one of the least understood and most often neglected elements of the business plan. It is also one of the most difficult to prepare and one of the major keys to your business's success.

Selling is a part of your marketing procedure. You won't have a business if you don't sell anything and chances are you won't sell anything if you don't market it properly. And the way to proper marketing lies in the preparation of a detailed marketing plan.

So if marketing is not selling, just what is marketing?

Marketing
Basically, marketing consists of identifying the need for your product or service and then presenting the goods or services at the right time, place and price to satisfy the need. This is usually done by identifying your potential customers and selecting the right advertising and promotional methods to make the market aware of your goods or services. In a nutshell, that's about it. Sounds simple enough but getting it right can be extremely difficult.

202

The SWOT analysis

The first step in preparing your marketing plan should be to undertake what is known as a SWOT analysis. This is an acronym for: *Strengths, Weaknesses, Opportunities* and *Threats*.

Take a sheet of blank paper and draw a line down the middle. On one side of the line list your strengths. Are you personally well known and respected in the marketplace? What is it about your product or service that makes it stand out from the crowd? List any unique selling features or benefits that you will have over your competitors, *e.g. Only hardware shop in the area where Chinese is spoken,* that type of thing.

On the other side of the line, list your weaknesses. For example, limited capital, not known in the marketplace, limited buying capacity, etc. Repeat this exercise for your opportunities and threats. Opportunities are gaps in the market or weaknesses your competitors have that you can exploit and take advantage of. Threats could be things like the dropping of tariff protection to allow cheap imports onto the market or changes to government legislation that could affect your trading and so on.

In compiling your SWOT analysis, list every strength, weakness, opportunity and threat you can think of (no matter how obscure) and then undertake finer analysis later on. You will find this exercise very useful in helping to produce your final marketing plan.

A properly presented formal marketing plan will not only assist you greatly in raising finance, it will provide a blueprint for your growth and ongoing success. It should encompass all the aspects of your overall marketing strategy and can be best summarised by looking at what is known as:

The six Ps of marketing

product, price, packaging, promotion, place and prospects.

- *product* - what you are going to sell
- *price* - at what price you are going to sell it
- *packaging* - how you are going to present it to the market
- *promotion* - how you are going to promote it
- *place* - where you are going to sell it (distribution method)
- *prospects* - who you are going to sell it to.

Your marketing plan should also include the following aspects:

- *market research*
- *details of the market*
- *current state of the market*
- *competition and pricing policies*
- *advertising and promotional strategies.*

Let's take a closer look at each of these items.:

Market research
This should consist of a comprehensive analysis of the market you are going to enter into. It should include a brief history of the market as well as elements like the overall growth of demand in recent years and increases or decreases in the number of competitors. This type of information is available from a number of sources, including trade and professional associations, the Australian Bureau of Statistics (ABS) and other people in your chosen industry.

You should also attempt to talk to as many potential clients as possible and indicate reasons why they would be likely to use your services or products in preference to their present suppliers. Try to get your information from as many different *reliable* sources as possible. It is very dangerous to rely too heavily on information gathered from a small section of the marketplace.

There are many cases of businesses that have got themselves into trouble through poor market research; let me give you an example:

Many years ago I worked for a large trading company that held a number of agencies for a wide range of products. They were a very diversified organisation and were always on the lookout for new opportunities. At one stage, one of the company's suppliers in America offered us a new line: a range of very up-market corn cob pipes.

According to the US company, these were a really hot item and they were selling very well in America. A sample range was called for and the sales manager for that division took the range into one of the large wholesalers, a company called Hoffnungs. The buyer there was most enthusiastic and ordered several thousand pipes. The sales manager was highly elated and reported back to the office that we had indeed discovered a great new line. The same day the company sent off an order for tens of thousands of pipes.

Some time later, they approached some of the other wholesalers but couldn't get another order. After doing the rounds of virtually every other wholesaler in Australia without success, the sales manager was totally mystified and eventually asked one of the buyers, "Look, this is a fantastic range, why won't you give me an order?"

The buyer replied, "All the wholesalers I know of buy their corn cob pipes direct from America. The only one I know that doesn't is Hoffnungs, why don't you try them?"

You can see what had happened. The company had based its entire market research on just one buyer's reaction! It might seem like a particularly stupid thing to do but this is a true story. Perhaps not surprisingly, the company concerned eventually got into deep trouble and went broke. *Included in the receiver's inventory was a very large quantity of corn cob pipes!*

That story is not an isolated case and the corporate history books are full of similar disasters. Make sure you do your market research thoroughly. You should consider enlisting professional help from a market research firm. If you can't afford professional help, you can try doing the market research yourself. Talk to your potential customers and ask lots of questions. Try to find out exactly what the market wants. Is there something they are not getting from your competitors that you can supply? Remember to list details of any sources of information used for your research in the appendices of your business plan.

Details of the market

Finding and identifying your market niche is extremely important. You must identify which area of the market you can best serve. In preparing your marketing plan it is important to remember not to try to be all things to all people; this is a certain recipe for failure. Identify the precise area of the market you are going to concentrate on and utilise your resources to their greatest effect. Very few businesses can tackle every area of a market and survive.

For instance, let's say you were planning to start a carpet retailing business in a major city. You could start by looking at the overall market for carpet in Australia. This type of information is available from the Australian Bureau of Statistics. These figures may include commercial premises, clubs, government departments, etc. It would also include all types of quality and price ranges, from the cheapest to the luxury end of the market. You then need to try to break this down to the specific section of the market you are going to cater to.

For example, you might choose to target the commercial market in the central business district or the upper end of the domestic market in the eastern suburbs, etc. Once you have identified the market segment you are aiming at, you then need to incorporate this into the rest of your business strategy. Your plan should aim towards you becoming recognised as the specialist for the particular segment you have chosen.

The area of the market you choose to service will determine such things as your location. Correctly identifying your potential customer's socio-economic grouping will also determine your promotional strategy and your choice of media. Your target audience is known as your *Prime Prospect Profile* (PPP) in advertising jargon.

For instance, is your target market commercially based or are they mainly domestic consumers? If so, are they housewives over 35 years old or are they working mothers or teenagers or is it a combination of a number of different groups? The ABS can also help in identifying geographically where your PPPs can be found. They can even supply you with a colour coded map, showing the geographical location and main concentration of your potential market.

State of the market
Once you have identified your market niche, you should give a brief overview of the current state of the market you are going to enter. For instance, do you think the market is going to grow or is currently under-catered to? Wherever possible present evidence to support your claims. Make sure your target sales figures are realistic, based on your analysis of the market and future prospects and trends. You should also make sure that the market you are entering is not just a passing fad and that there are real prospects for long term growth. Include any information you have on reasons for this growth and its sustainability.

For instance, in the case of the carpet retailer, you could include

206

industry projections on the number of new dwellings or renovations being undertaken in your chosen geographical area. The ABS or your local council should be able to assist with this information or you could try the Master Builders Association or the Real Estate Institute. The secret of good market research lies in being able to track down sources of information that can assist with your future projections.

Competition and pricing policies
Supply as much information as you can gather on your competitors and include clippings of their press ads, etc., in your appendices. What will be their reaction to your entering the marketplace? Are they likely to try to undercut you or try to force you out of business? What are your major strengths? How will you overcome your weaknesses? Will you be cheaper, better, more convenient, more reliable or a combination of these things? What is your marketing edge? What are your *Unique Selling Points* (USPs)? If you are planning to be cheaper, how will you achieve this? What is your leverage? Can you buy as well or better than the competition?

Note: If you have any obvious weaknesses you should point these out, including your plans of how you intend to overcome them. For instance: we will not be the cheapest on the market, however, we will be the only company within a 20-kilometre radius offering this service or we intend to give free in-home service, etc.

Advertising and promotional strategy
How will you advertise and which media will you use? Are you going to be involved in trade shows, will you need printed literature, how much will it cost? What percentage of your overall sales budget will be spent on advertising? What is your competitors' advertising policy and how do you plan to match it or better it?
(See chapter - Advertising)

Summary
Once you have prepared your marketing strategy, make sure you monitor and review it constantly. Also, if you are employing staff, make sure that they understand exactly what your marketing objectives are. If they are going to help you to realise your goals, it is important that they also know exactly what you are trying to achieve.

YOUR GOALS

SECTION FIVE:

GOAL SETTING

AND

GETTING HELP

33. THE FIVE STEPS TO SUCCESS

"The most important thing about goals is having one."
Geoffrey Abert

Most people at some stage would have been exposed in one form or another to some of the ideas and principles of goal setting. This could have been in business, at school, at a course or by simply reading a book or watching a video tape. Chances are most of it was good advice based on sound principles and ideas.

The problem with goal setting is, it works in different ways for different people. Often the way it is presented gives the impression that it is some form of alternative religion or a panacea for everybody's problems and woes. This can be especially true if the presenter is one of those high powered American motivational speakers who sometimes come across as 'born again' evangelists. The result is that people have trouble knowing where the hype ends and the truth starts.

Over the years, I have attended a good many courses and seminars on goal setting and I have read numerous books on the subject. From my own experience, I have condensed the main principles down into five simple steps. I firmly believe if you follow these steps, there isn't much in life that you can't achieve.

Here they are:

Step 1: Know what you want

This may sound stupid but one of the main reasons why most people don't get what they want out of life is because they don't really know what it is they want. Think about it for a moment.

Do you know exactly what you hope to achieve out of life both in the short and long term?

I have asked this question of many individuals and groups and found that when you really get down to it, very few people are able to answer with a precise definition of exactly what they hope to achieve in life. Few have a clear picture of where they are going or where they would like to be. Most people drift fairly aimlessly through life with no clear plan, taking things largely as they come. They tend to react to what happens to them, rather than trying to change the circumstances around them and take control. Try asking a few people yourself exactly what it is they want to achieve in life. Most will answer in vague terms with statements like, "Well, I would like lots of money!" This is not a clear goal. *Precisely how much do you want and what are you going to use it for when you get it?*

They will often add as an explanation, something like, "Well, I'd like to travel." *Not good enough!* Where do you want to travel to? When do you want to go? How long do you want to stay there and what are you going to do when you get there? Can you see the difference? You have a much better chance of achieving your goals if you have a clear picture in your mind of exactly what it is you want. *You'll see it when you believe it!*

You will find it helpful if you write your goals down. Some people like to carry these around with them in their wallet or purse. They may even go so far as to carry a picture of their holiday destination or dream home or car with them at all times. Some like to stick this up on the wall in a prominent position so that they can see it every day, so that when they feel discouraged they can look at it and it spurs them on. I recommend any of these steps as helpful but only if you feel comfortable with them. If you don't, then don't bother. The main thing is to have a clear picture in your mind of exactly what you want.

What the mind can conceive and believe, it can achieve!

Step 2: Know when you want it

People often confuse goal setting with dreaming. Let me say right here and now there's absolutely nothing wrong with dreaming! In the words of that famous song from South Pacific: "You've got to have a dream, if you don't have a dream, how are you going to have a dream come true?" The major difference between a dream and a goal is simple: *A goal is a dream with a date on it.*

Once you have decided what it is you want, your next step is to decide when you are going to get it. Your goals should also be realistic and achievable. That doesn't mean to say that you have to aim low, but it may mean that you have to break your major goal down into a series of smaller ones. For instance, if you are working in the mail room at BHP, there is not much point in saying you want to be managing director of the company within six months. However, you could say that you would like to be head of the department within one year and then say, a branch manager within five years and a state manager within ten years. Then, general manager in fifteen years and managing director in twenty years.

The beauty of breaking your big goal down into lots of minor goals is this: each time you achieve a minor goal along the way, you get the feeling of winning and being one step closer to the major target and this gives you momentum. Somebody once said, "the best way to eat an elephant is one bite at a time"!

Be prepared to review your goals, especially your long-term ones. You might set yourself a goal for five years from now with reviews every six months. You could then assess your progress at each stage and adjust your goal time upwards or downwards, depending upon progress.

Step 3: Develop a plan

Once you have decided exactly what it is that you want and set yourself a time frame for achieving it, your next step is to devise a concrete plan of action.

I remember once going to a seminar conducted by a very fast talking London cockney entrepreneur. He told us that if you wanted to own a Rolls Royce, your best bet was to go down to the Rolls Royce showroom every day and get into the car and sniff the leather seats and imagine yourself driving around in it. According to his philosophy, if you did this long enough you would definitely end up owning a Roller! Well, I might be a cynic but I think if you went around sniffing car seats, about the only thing that would happen to you is you would get arrested! Visualisation can be a big help but if you want to become rich, you will need to do a lot more than just think about it.

Another popular theory is the 'positive affirmation' theory. This method usually involves having a goal written down and saying it to yourself over and over again every morning as you look at yourself in the mirror to shave or put on your makeup, like some sort of Buddhist chant. This may work quite well for some people and I am not knocking it. However, I think the most likely way you are going to achieve your goals is to develop a practical, believable plan and then work as hard as you can towards achieving it. Thorough planning is the secret of successful goal setting.

Your plan is simply your map of how you are going to arrive at your destination. Sit down with a piece of paper and a pencil and work it out. If it is at all practical, involve your partner or family and friends and tell them what it is you want to achieve and ask them to give you suggestions as to how you can go about it. You will also be encouraged when these people ask you how you are going with your plan and it will help to drive you along.

Step 4: Don't be afraid to go for it

Sadly, many people go through life not realising their full potential simply because they feel they wouldn't be able to achieve the things they want. How often have you heard someone say something like, "I would like to have been a teacher but I didn't have the education" or "I wanted to be a lawyer but my family were against it"? This is invariably an excuse for their own lack of effort or dedication.

It is far easier to blame our parents for our short comings than admit to our own lack of commitment. There are also those people who have very low self-esteem and simply feel they are unworthy of a better position in life. *Don't let yourself or anybody else talk you out of being anything less than what you want to be.*

Step 5: Believe in yourself

Visualise yourself doing what it is you want to do. Develop a *'can-do'* attitude. Imagine yourself visiting the places you want to go to or driving the car you would like to drive or living in the home you would like to own. If you have a workable, believable plan, you will find this easy to do. Develop a strong belief in yourself and your ability. Accept your faults and weaknesses (nobody is perfect) and learn to like yourself.

Mix with positive people and high achievers. If you mix with people who have a losing attitude and low self esteem, sooner or later you will find yourself falling into step with them. There's an old theory that says, "If you put a crab in a bucket it will climb out. But if you put two crabs in a bucket, neither of them can climb out because one keeps pulling the other one back down". Mix with high achievers and you will find them encouraging and reassuring you along the way.

Summary

Whatever it is you set out to achieve, keep at it until you get there. It is often said that, *"You can lead a horse to water but you can't make it drink"*. That is simply not true! If you stand there long enough, the horse will eventually get thirsty and drink. It's simply a matter of time and persistence.

I like what Calvin Coolidge (the former U.S. President) had to say about persistence:

> *"Nothing in the world can take the place of persistence.*
> *Talent will not; nothing is more common than unsuccessful*
> *men with talent. Genius will not; unrewarded genius is*
> *almost a proverb. Education will not; the world is full of*
> *educated derelicts. Persistence and determination are*
> *omnipotent. The slogan 'press on' has solved and always*
> *will solve the problems of the human race."*

If you believe in yourself and you keep at it, there isn't much in life that you can't achieve.

THE FIVE STEPS TO SUCCESS

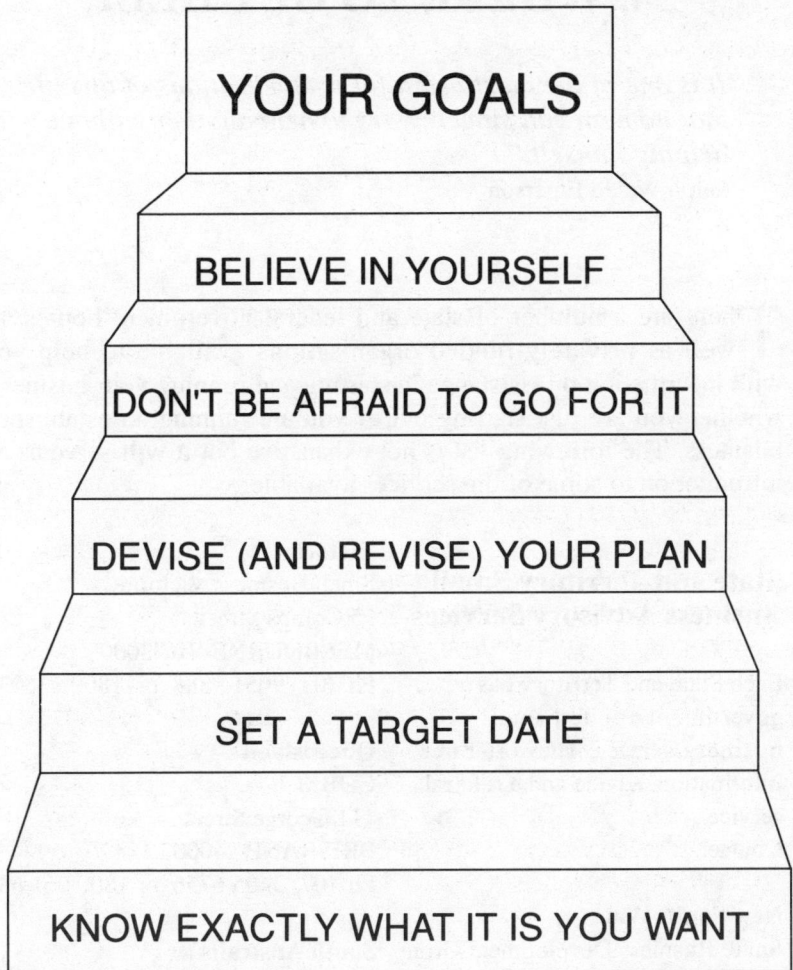

YOUR GOALS

BELIEVE IN YOURSELF

DON'T BE AFRAID TO GO FOR IT

DEVISE (AND REVISE) YOUR PLAN

SET A TARGET DATE

KNOW EXACTLY WHAT IT IS YOU WANT

34. WHERE TO GET HELP

"It is one of the most beautiful compensations of this life that no man can sincerely try to help another without helping himself."
Ralph Waldo Emerson

There are a number of state and federal government bodies, as well as privately-funded organisations available to help you with information or assistance in starting and running your business, whether you are just starting out or you are running an established business. The following list is not exhaustive but it will serve as an introduction to some of the services available.

State and Territory Small Business Advisory Services

Each State and Territory has a government-funded small business service. They offer free information, advice and a referral service.
Contact:

New South Wales
Small Business Development Group
225 George Street
SYDNEY 2000
Ph. (02) 9242 6684 or 1800 132 846

Victoria
Small Business Victoria
55 Collins Street
MELBOURNE VIC 3000
Ph. (03) 9651 9888 or 1800 136034

Queensland
GOBIS
111 George Street
BRISBANE 4000
Ph. (07) 3405 6756 or 1800 061 631

South Australia
The Business Centre
145 South Terrace
ADELAIDE 5000
Ph. (08) 8233 4600 or 1800 188 018

Western Australia
Small Business Development
Corporation
553 Hay Street
PERTH WA 6000
Ph. (08) 9220 0222 or 1800 199125

Tasmania
Regional Business Development
Small Business
22 Elizabeth Street
HOBART TAS 7000
Ph. (03) 6233 5712 or 1800 005 262

Australian Capital Territory
ACT Business Link
12a Thesiger Court
DEAKIN   ACT 2600
Ph. (06) 282 2199

Northern Territory
Small Business Advisory Services
76 The Esplanade
DARWIN NT 0800
Ph. (08) 8999 7916

Business Licence Centres

Most states and territories now have
business licence centres which offer
intending and existing business
operators a one stop point of enquiry
through which information and
application forms for state business
licences can be obtained.

New South Wales
Business Licence Information
Service
175 Castlereagh Street
SYDNEY 2000
Ph. (02) 9286 0099 or 1800 463 976

Victoria
Business Licence Centre
55 Collins Street
MELBOURNE VIC 3000
Ph. (03) 9651 9888 or 1800 136034

Queensland
Qld Business Licence Info. Centre
111 George Street
BRISBANE   4000
Ph. (07) 3405 6756 or 1800 061 631

Western Australia
Business Licence Information
553 Hay Street
PERTH 6000
Ph. (08) 9220 0234

217

South Australia
Business Licence Information
145 South Terrace
ADELAIDE 5000
(08)8233 4650

Australian Capital Territory
Operates from NSW Business
Licence Information Service
Ph. 1800 463 976

Tasmania
Business Licence Information Centre
22 Elizabeth Street
HOBART TAS 7000
Ph. (03) 6233 5712 or 1800 005 262

AUS INDUSTRY

There are a number of different departments, offering a wide range of help to small business in various areas at federal, state and territory levels.

Unfortunately, they seem to continually change their names, addresses and telephone numbers and keeping up with them is virtually a full time job. In what can only be described as an unbelievable act of common sense, the government has finally seen fit to establish a hot line number that can supply information on the various services. It is called the AUSINDUSTRY HOT LINE and the number is:

13 28 46

It list all the government support programs available such as research and development grants, export market develop assistance, networking, quality management, environmental management and business planning. They even promise to mail out printed information within 24 hours!

There's also a CD ROM available listing all the services. What's more, just to make sure it really works, I rang the number and they answered straight away. Fantastic. This will certainly save you a lot of time and effort. Well done!

Chambers of Commerce

The Australian Chamber of Commerce represents the interests of the State and Territorial Chambers at a national level on a broad range of issues ranging from monitoring legislation that affects private enterprise, to assistance and advice concerning employer and employee relations. Chambers of Commerce at the state, territorial and regional level provide a wide range of services that assist small business. These include:

• Business support activities such as business and legal advisory services, industrial relations services, award updates and dispute settlement.

• Skill development activities include training, workshops, small business forums, regional forums, library and research facilities.

• International trade activities including business matching, trade sourcing, trade information, import and export opportunities and a tariff advisory service.

• Networking opportunities are available through trade functions and overseas missions.

In most states, the Chamber of Commerce also sponsors a Small Business Association or Advisory Service which focuses on the needs and development of the small business sector in its state, providing access to professional advice.

The ACT Chamber of Commerce & Industry

2 Kembla street
FYSHWICK ACT 2609
Ph. (06) 280 5029

New South Wales

State Chamber of Commerce and Industry
93 York Street
SYDNEY NSW 2000
Ph. (02) 9290 5400

Victoria

Victorian Employers' Chamber of Commerce and Industry
50 Burwood Road
HAWTHORN VIC 3122
Ph. (03) 9810 6333

Queensland

Qld Chamber of Commerce and Industry
375 Wickham Terrace
BRISBANE QLD 4000
Ph. (07) 3831 1699

Western Australia

Chamber of Commerce and Industry of WA
190 Hay Street
EAST PERTH WA 6004
Ph. (09) 365 7555

WHERE TO GET HELP

South Australia
SA Employers' Chamber of
Commerce and Industry
136 Greenhill Road
UNLEY SA 5061
Ph. (08) 373 1422

Tasmania
Tasmanian Chamber of Commerce
& Industry
30 Burnett Street
North Hobart Tas 7000
Ph. (002) 34 5933

Northern Territory
NT Chamber of Commerce
& Industry
2 Shepherd Street
DARWIN NT 0800
Ph. (089) 81 5755

**Australia Chamber of
Commerce and Industry**
Canberra Secretariat
24 Brisbane Avenue
BARTON ACT 2600
Ph. (06) 273 2311

Business Enterprise Centres

Business in the Community Ltd., was established in the mid 1980s to provide a mechanism for local job creation and the economic growth of small business at a community level.

To achieve its objectives, BCL has established a number of Business Enterprise Centres (BECs) whose main role is to help small businesses. It does this through the provision of a free advisory and counselling service both to people wishing to start up their own business and those already in business.

Other activities often provided by the centres include skills training courses, seminars and workshops, and managed workspaces (also known as 'incubators'), which provide on-site management and a range of services on a short-term leasing basis.

BECs are now established in NSW, Victoria, South Australia, Western Australia, Tasmania, ACT and the Northern Territory. At time of writing, there were none in Qld but this may change soon. Check you local phone book.

The BECs are a terrific organisa-tion and you will find them most helpful and most of their services are free.

For regional addresses of the Business Enterprise Centres, consult you local telephone book or call the head office in your state, as follows:

New South Wales.
Business in the Community Ltd
1/ 382 Victoria Avenue
Chatswood 2067
Ph. (02) 9413 3230

Victoria
Business in the Community Ltd
50 Burwood Road
Hawthorn 3122
Ph. (03) 9819 6210

Western Australia
Business in the Community Ltd
5/1275 Hay Street
West Perth 6005
Ph. (09) 322 3387

South Australia
Business in the Community Inc.
5/182 Victoria Square
Adelaide 5000
PH. (08) 8226 2806

Northern Territory
Business in the Community Ltd
PO Box 37192
Winnellie 0821
Ph. (08) 8941 1339

Tasmania
Mentor Resources Tasmania
25 Hunter street
HOBART TAS 7000
Ph. (002) 335 448

Chamber of Manufacturers

There are a number of industry employer organisations providing advice and assistance to small manufacturers in key areas, ranging from industrial relations, legislation and regulations, to international and domestic trade, finance and business management.
The type and level of assistance varies from organisation to organisation and from state to state but can include such things as:

- *Taxation and financial Services*
- *Legal advice*
- *Industrial relations advice*
- *Environment services*
- *Business advisory services*

Listed below are some of the major organisations in each state and territory.

New South Wales
Australian Business Ltd
3/140 Arthur Street
NORTH SYDNEY NSW 2060
Ph. (02) 9927 7500

ACT Branch of above:
MMI Building
78 Northbourne Ave
Canberra City ACT 2608
Ph. (06) 248 6477

(Note: They also has offices in major regional country areas).

221

Victoria
The Australian Chamber of
Manufactures (Vic Division)
380 St Kilda Rd
MELBOURNE VIC 3004
Ph. (03) 9698 4111 or 1800 33 1103.

Queensland
Qld Chamber Commerce & Industry
375 Wickham Terrace
BRISBANE QLD 4000
PH. (07) 3842 2244

Western Australia
Chamber of Commerce and Ind.
190 Hay Street
EAST PERTH WA 6004
Ph. (09) 365 7555

South Australia
SA Employers' Chamber of
Commerce and Industry
136 Greenhill Road
UNLEY SA 5061
Ph. (08) 373 1422

Tasmania
Tasmanian Chamber of Commerce
& Industry
30 Burnett Street
North Hobart Tas 7000
Ph. (002) 34 5933

Northern Territory
NT Confederation of Com & Ind.
2 Shepherd Street
Darwin NT 0800
Ph. (089) 81 5755

The Australian Bureau of Statistics (ABS)

The ABS offers a range of statistical information to assist small business. This includes maps of the most likely place to locate your business. They can also provide detailed information on the best location for your target market.

New South Wales
3rd Floor, St Andrews House
Sydney Square
SYDNEY NSW 2000
inquiries (02) 9268 4611
bookshop (02) 9268 4620
fax (02) 9268 4668

Tasmania
200 Collins Street
HOBART TAS 7000
inquiries (03) 6222 5800
bookshop (03) 6222 5973
fax (03) 6222 5995

Victoria
Level 5, 485 La Trobe Street
MELBOURNE VIC 3000
inquiries (03) 9615 7755
bookshop (03) 9615 7974
fax (03) 9615 7798

Australian Capital Territory
9th floor FAI House
197 London Circuit
CANBERRA CITY 2601
inquiries (06) 252 6627
bookshop (06) 207 0326
fax (06) 207 0282

Queensland
18th Floor
313 Adelaide Street
BRISBANE QLD 4000
inquiries (07) 3222 6351
bookshop (07) 3222 6350
fax (07) 3229 6283

Western Australia
Level 16, Exchange Plaza
2 The Esplanade
PERTH WA 6000
inquiries (09) 360 5140
bookshop (09) 360 5307
fax (09) 360 5955

South Australia
55 Currie Street
ADELAIDE SA 5000
inquiries (08) 8237 7100
bookshop (08) 8237 7582
fax (08) 8237 7566

Northern Territory
5th Floor, AANT Building
81 Smith Street
DARWIN NT 0800
inquiries (08) 8943 2111
fax (08) 8981 1 218

The author of this book Peter Thorpe, is a sought after public speaker and trainer. Why not hire Peter for your next seminar or workshop?

For further information about rates and availability, contact:

PETER THORPE MARKETING
7th floor 8 Kippax Street
SURRY HILLS NSW 2010
TEL: (02) 9282 6937
FAX: (02) 9211 2359

A division of
The Advertising Department Pty. Ltd.
ACN 003 519 631